Jesus Means Freedom

ERNST KÄSEMANN

Jesus Means Freedom

A polemical survey of the New Testament

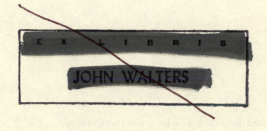
SCM PRESS LTD

To my wife and children

Translated by Frank Clarke from the German
Der Ruf der Freiheit
(third, revised, edition) J. C. B. Mohr (Paul Siebeck),
Tübingen 1968

334 00775 5

First published in English 1969
by SCM Press Ltd
56 Bloomsbury Street London WC 1

Printed in Great Britain by
Northumberland Press Limited
Gateshead

CONTENTS

TRANSLATOR'S NOTE

This book is, of course, written against a German background and contains some, though not many, references to events in the history of the church in Germany during the past forty years. As the story of the Confessing Church, with its synods at Barmen and Dahlem, the Nazi persecution of the church and the involvement of members of the church, including Dietrich Bonhoeffer, are now becoming well known, I have not added explanatory footnotes. Further details are readily available in one of the many studies of the period.

F.C.

PREFACE

This little book is a contribution, of a polemical nature, to the present discussion of the New Testament and modern theology. It was occasioned in the first place by the incessant attacks on myself and my views from the so-called 'Confessing Movement' after my lecture on 'The Presence of the Crucified One' at the German *Kirchentag* in Hanover in 1967, and it was intended especially for church members who were interested in theology, because they are the people who are most in need of information about primitive Christianity and the results of our research. The fact that a third edition has been called for within a few months has given me an opportunity to make certain drastic changes. By writing, I have freed myself from the anger that originally brought me to work on the subject, but the fire is still smoking just a little. It may perhaps obviate unjustified interpretations if I state categorically that I do not regret one single sentence of what I first wrote; on the contrary, I still stand without qualification by the whole of it, including the cool, calculating, and not too polite turns of speech which German literature has never lacked, even at the highest level. Why, indeed, should one not be satisfied in retrospect with one's work? James 1.25 even promises us that 'a doer that acts . . . shall be blessed in his doing'. But prolonged stormy weather is depressing, whereas thunder and lightning, if they are soon over, clear the air. I simply do not want any longer to go round wrangling with the people in Germany who pose as guardians of Bible and confession. That is petty and small-minded, unprofitable and wearisome, as old popular methods of combating heresy are bound to lose their edge.

But it must not be overlooked that the so-called 'Confessing Movement' has the merit of bringing to light the crisis that exists in the church in Germany, as indeed throughout the world. In spite of all the outcry that is being raised today, that crisis is by no means new, though at present it is in a special way acute. The conflict over the challenge of freedom runs all through the church's history, and it has constantly to be taken up again in every generation and in every Christian life. The dividing lines that sometimes seem to separate old and young, groups and denominations, never cease to shift. They really mark the place where now, as formerly, both conversion and impenitence are found, and the old Adam wrestles with the new. Christian freedom is bestowed, not stolen; it is endured rather than learnt. In any case it is not acquired once for all; it comes to meet us and remains ahead of us. Indeed, in changing situations it changes its form and watchword. It is always changing us, and we may not and must not remain the same when it takes us into its service. But no one likes to change of his own accord; there are always traditions to which one can appeal so as to protect oneself from present freedom, and there are always utopias in whose airy expanses one can seek shelter, so as not to have to stand one's ground on earth. But it is vital for every faith that we accept freedom's challenge today. Anyone who does not comprehend it and lay hold of it is just throwing the game away. I am sure that the root cause of the present world-wide crisis of the church is that the Christian world has thrown away too much of the freedom with which it has been endowed and to which it is being called.

That is where we all have to start afresh, and if we start from there, even our theological controversy acquires meaning and dignity. It is conducted in this little book by means of an analysis of the New Testament writings; there is, of course, no attempt at completeness; and perhaps the omission of recondite argument may appeal to a fairly wide circle of readers. The expert will notice where I am indebted to others, either in agreement or in disagreement. What I have tried to do is to put things in perspective and to point out the emphasis needed for research. I see the whole of the New Testament as involving the cause of Christian freedom, and I have done my best to show that that cause is developed in much diversity, because it exists only in terms of practical mundane affairs, in relation to Christian selflessness, stupidity, misrepresentation and denial, and changes its spearhead from time to time. Like God's faithfulness, the gospel is new every morning and has been heard in many tongues ever since Pentecost, although ecclesiastical convenience has tried to turn the Holy Spirit into a single gramophone record, and makes the human spirit nothing more than a loudspeaker.

This means that we cannot renounce controversy in theology. So long as we are not in heaven, the challenge of freedom is always controversial, a cause of vexation both to the Christian church and to ourselves. In contrast to the former editions of my work, however, I have with some difficulty set narrow limits to my discussion of the present controversy. The earlier preface and postscript, as well as all kinds of attacks from the cover of some problematical question or other, have been sacrificed to objectivity. Perhaps this makes the attack, on the whole, more concentrated. I hope that stylistic improvements and various additions, especially a new chapter dealing with the Epistle to the Hebrews and Lucan theology, have also helped. I had no intention of writing an academic treatise. There is a time and a historical place for everything, although scholars sometimes imagine, or give the impression, that they alone stand apart from transitory things. It is certainly true that no one can talk about Christian freedom except in so far as it gives rise to a larger or smaller measure of his own experience, or even of his own lack of comprehension; least of all is it possible here to conceal one's personal involvement. My generation has been able to gather an unusual amount of experience in this respect. Like life itself, it was mostly painful; and at the same time it was uncommonly instructive in illuminating the circumstances of early Christianity. Taken in conjunction with New Testament analysis it makes it possible to draw up something like a theological sum. Before we quit the field, we may once more hoist the signal under which we formed up. Cromwell whispered on his death-bed : 'I know that I was once in grace.' In spite of the preacher (Eccles. 1.2, etc.), not all was vanity!

Tübingen, Easter 1968   ERNST KÄSEMANN

The Theme

What is the essential nature of the church? We must not suppose that either the world or the 'general public' bothers about such a question today, although, strangely enough, the radio still allots a surprising amount of its time to it. It would even be a mistake to suggest, for example, on the anniversary of the Reformation, that our generation is loudly asking, not so much whether there is a God of grace, as whether there is a God at all. Quite apart from the fact that, outside ideological and perhaps traditional philosophical problems, it is only in the form of the first of these questions that the second makes sense, we have to take care continually not to indulge in wishful thinking and conceit. Religiosity and its associations are not likely to die out as long as human beings exist, and Christians will bear that in mind in one way or another without making much capital out of it for themselves. They ought to know from experience that this state of affairs is very puzzling and always equivocal. But a sober judgment about our situation compels us to admit that western Christianity and our German church in its present circumstances are bygone forms of life. We may dispute whether and how far they can be resuscitated, how intensively we ought to summon them up and exert ourselves about them, or whether (taking a course of which I should personally disapprove) we should without more ado take final leave of them. In any case it is obvious that we cannot rely on them any longer, that we shall have to abandon them before long, and that our church leaders' most urgent task ought to be to prepare reception camps and emergency huts for the occasion. We ought to consider what it is absolutely essential to preserve, and what we must therefore adapt ourselves to, here and now, with complete concentration. I think it is desirable and appropriate simply to ask how people can be kept together or reached afresh. On their account, reduction, demolition, and shifting of emphasis in all the existing and constantly growing church institutions is unavoidable.

However that may be, the necessary analysis of our situation will have to start from a basic recognition of the fact that our everyday life is determined by a practical, unproblematical atheism which is by no means rebellious. For many reasons, rational and irrational, Christianity in this country is still exceptionally favoured. It rarely represents a decisive spiritual potential; people make use of it because it is useful, no more and no less. That is done by individuals who do not know what other setting to provide for their working day and for the important events of their lives. It is done, too, by the state, the parties, and their offshoots, for the sake of those innumerable individuals and the organizations that represent them. If this is true, the function of Christendom in the life of our people, whatever their own thoughts and wishes may be, is limited to the preservation, strengthening, and as far as possible the increase of the existing internal order within the social, and perhaps even the political sphere. We need not despise this; indeed, we must support it as far as we can. We all fare better where a right ordering is striven for and achieved, and the church must not feel that it is too good to lend a hand. In some circumstances, service in things temporal may be evidence that the church is guided by things eternal. Revolution for its own sake and at any price is always anti-Christian, however hard such a maxim may seem to youthful rebels. The conservative attitude is both justified and necessary—a fact which many of us disregard and which the church must acknowledge and allow freely, especially when it is unpopular to do so. Everyone ought to be clear that we are not undermining authority as the basis of a practicable order; on the contrary, we want it and support it, without shying at the displeasure and disappointment of those who think differently.

But these preliminary remarks merely mark off the area within which our questions, anxieties, predicaments, and not least our 'Protestantism'—i.e., our opposition to existing realities and unrealities—are aroused. A conservative attitude may be a possibility and a necessity in our service. But it does not constitute the essential nature of the church. To preserve and strive for order in the social sphere, and, if the way is open, in the political sphere, to lend our services to the state, the parties and their offshoots as auxiliaries and emergency helpers, does not injure our dignity. But that holds good only as long as we do not, by so acting, lend colour to the malicious saying (unfortunately often enough and for long enough true) that religion is the opium of the people. Here our enjoyment, our service, our inclination for authority, cease abruptly, and it is a discredit to the whole body of Christians in our nation that in this regard those things have not ceased, but continue their undisturbed course, cheerful, satisfied, and un-Protestant, into things sacred and profane. Taken in detail, the effect may be small. Taken in the lump, it is remarkably great, and that is why public bodies support it. For Christianity itself the effect is deadly. Every word, every deed, every demonstration is a denial of our Lord and ourselves, unless we test them from the point of view of whether they are opium of the people, or can be regarded and abused as such.

Here we ought no longer to trouble the old lady, the child, and the plain man, who might well expect us to help them in their burdensome existence, to comfort them, and to speak in language that they understand. We cannot relieve any of those people from their responsibility for facing their own death and preparing for it. Only doctors are allowed to give opiates to people who are suffering or dying, and pastors have no business to go poaching on their preserves. Otherwise, instead of helping people, they might finish them off, and in fact there have been innumerable victims of religious opiates that were offered with the best intentions. Ought we not just to think about this, and feel a sharp twinge of conscience when present-day theology is accused of leading students astray, con-

fusing simple people, and depriving them of faith? As if faith
consisted in hearing what one expects as a matter of course
in divine service, and what is felt at least by ourselves, if not
by the world, to be tolerable. We cry murder without noticing
that creeping death is at work everywhere. While we extol
rebirth, we forget that it presupposes a dying that is new every
day and goes down into the very depths of our being, as well
as a living despair of our own godliness. Anyone who does not
discern, and hate, and oppose the old Adam in the church
really ought not to be shocked by its continuance outside the
church. Where mere edification and boredom spread themselves, there can be no resounding gospel message, even if
the whole Bible has been read aloud.

In view of these considerations, we ask whether the church
itself knows how things stand with regard to its essential nature.
Can the church define this nature sharply, in a single word or
sentence, so that all other questions and answers are brought
into the context of such definition? At the same time, that
means that such a statement must not be shaped to the fancy
of the individual or of a confession, but that it must be common to all and must be their final standard of judgment. Consequently, it also represents the limits of unity, just as on the
same basis the existing separations can be seen in perspective,
differences and contrasts in faith and action tolerated, and
compromises concluded. No one who knows anything about the
history of the church and its denominations will have much
hope of seeing anything more than a rapprochement in the
spheres of dogmatics, liturgy, constitution, or indeed of canon
law. Even a recourse to early Christianity and the New Testament remains problematical, because interpretations differ at
once; although without an attempt at such recourse, the importance attached to particular traditions would become paramount. Lastly, we have to take account of ethics, so far as it
does not relate simply to the present moment and its peremp-
tory requirements and expediencies – in short, to its immediate
short-term considerations. In ethics, Christian discipleship,
which otherwise appears as central and dominating, would

have to be subordinated to the question of one's perceptions and obligations in general.

It is obvious that Christians as a whole cannot for the most part offer any satisfactory solution to this. The best and most hopeful thing that can be said of their present situation is that they realize the problem and their own perplexity in relation to it; the usual answer that continues to hold the field is the proclamation of particular personal or denominational views. Over these it is possible to build human bridges; with them one can strive for, and indeed partly realize, organizational alliance and confederation. Yet they create our own dilemma in the ecumenical age, as it is called, when the truth of the gospel, no less than the credibility of us all in this world of ours, is at stake. In our situation, we can deal seriously with the true nature of the church only if the answer to such a question is simple and clear in three regards: the practice of Christian discipleship in the life of the individual, the basic doctrinal truth of the gospel, and the possibility and necessity of ecumenical union. Here we may conclude at once that any such union would have to be achieved, not merely by institutions, but by the Christian people, not from above, but by the so-called laity in all denominations and organizations. If it is put like that, it becomes clear, not only that such an undertaking is bound to seem absolutely hopeless, but also that everyone who takes any part in it knows that he is proclaiming a judgment on all the churches and on our collective personal piety, and that he therefore has to reckon with the power of the Holy Spirit and the reality of miracles.

None the less, there is for simple people a promise corresponding to the woes pronounced over the scribes and Pharisees, let alone the high officials who continue undisturbed their statements about the Holy Spirit, but make him a mysterious power instead of the herald and accomplisher of the simplest thing of all. The simplest thing that answers all the demands that have just been mentioned is the freedom of God's children. We shall discuss that in the following chapters, on the basis of the New Testament.

1 Was Jesus a 'liberal'?

I was told the following story in Amsterdam after the severe storms and floods from which Holland suffered in 1952. The scene was one of those parishes where people felt themselves strictly bound to obey God's commandments, and therefore to keep the Sabbath holy. The place was so threatened by wind and waves that the dyke had to be strengthened one Sunday if the inhabitants were to survive. The police notified the pastor, who now found himself in a religious difficulty. Should he call out the people of the parish that had been entrusted to him, and set them to do the necessary work, if it meant profaning the Sabbath? Should he, on the contrary, abandon them to destruction in order to honour the Sabbath? He found the burden of making a personal decision too much for him, and he summoned the church council to consult and decide. The discussion went as one might suppose: We live to carry out God's will. God, being omnipotent, can always perform a miracle with the wind and waves. Our duty is obedience, whether in life or in death. The pastor tried one last argument, perhaps against his own conviction: Did not Jesus himself, on occasion, break the fourth commandment and declare that the Sabbath was made for man, not man for the Sabbath? Thereupon a venerable old man stood up: 'I have always been troubled, Pastor, by something that I have never yet ventured to say publicly. Now I must say it. I have always had the feeling that our Lord Jesus was just a bit of a liberal.'

I do not know whether the story is *bien trouvé*, or whether it is literally true. Historians know that kind of thing much

less often than they themselves, as well as other people, think
they do. In any case, the story gives an excellent illustration
of a question that no Christian and no church can avoid,
although it is put in a banal form, and perhaps really is banal.
Was Jesus a 'liberal'? One has to answer Yes or No. To refrain
from asking the question, or to by-pass it with clever phrases,
or to answer it ambiguously, is to deny the real Jesus. Even if
individual Christians or churches back away from it personally,
however they may do so, they cannot escape the issue which
lies behind it. For the gospels do not leave us in the slightest
doubt that Jesus, judged by the standards of his religious environment, was in fact 'liberal', and that it was probably that
very fact that sent him to the cross. Here the most critical
history is on safe ground; here, if anywhere, knowledge and
gospel come together. We are therefore dealing with one of the
few things belonging most intimately to the 'saving facts' that
are often evoked today. We shall do well not to devalue this
plain and established 'fact', unless we want, as a matter of
course, to cast doubt on all the rest. If the history of Jesus has
any relevance at all, we cannot slink past this 'fact' without
endangering everything else and at least robbing it of its con-
crete relation to Jesus' life, and so making it unintelligible.

Was Jesus a 'liberal'? If the case is as it has been put forward
here, it is on the answer to this question that there depend
the truth and the saving power of discipleship, right and wrong
faith, judged by today's recognized standards both of conservative and critical theology and of congregational piety.
It is obviously a very inflammable matter, and one may perhaps see as clearly here as anywhere the force of Jesus' alleged
remark that has come down to us in an unfortunately, or
understandably, apocryphal writing: 'He who is near me is
near the fire, but he who is far from me is far from the Kingdom.' For the fact must not be overlooked or concealed that
the 'liberal' Jesus was a cause of offence, not only to his strictly
orthodox compatriots, but even to his first disciples, and that
the whole history of the church down to our own time reflects
a like annoyance at his peculiar freedom. His miracles and

resurrection may have been doubted. His 'liberal' attitude was
a constant thorn in the flesh for pious people, and for the most
part it was only sectarians who found it a reason for faith and
joy.

Does it cast a shadow on Jesus' devotion if we call him a
'liberal'? The question is absurd, although it is not only asked,
but answered in the affirmative. The abhorrence of liberalism,
and, connected with that, the fear felt by the orthodox, is
centuries old, and has not always been unfounded; in any case
it has been cultivated for a long time, and has lately become
a banner for world-wide ecclesiastical reaction. The deeper
question, inseparable from it, whether the Son of God may be
called 'liberal', may at first be put off for a time, because it has
to be given a more serious theological answer. It is a strange
position when 'devout' and 'liberal' are played off against each
other and one has to express an opinion for or against. But
today it is unmistakably plain that there cannot be the slightest
doubt of Jesus' devotion; and if the risk of omitting to say this
means that one may be pilloried for teaching a blasphemous
theology, it is better to make the point quite clear. I must, however, confess that what seems to me downright blasphemous is
to have to endorse Jesus' devotion. Nevertheless, in the circumstances I can hardly avoid doing so.

The historian, then, declares unreservedly that, as far as he
can judge, there is no room for doubt that Jesus took the
obligations of a devout Jew very seriously, even where the
Scriptures made no clear-cut demands, and that, for example,
he therefore hardly preached and worked beyond the borders
of Israel. There is no need to mention his going to the temple,
his prayers, his familiarity with the Old Testament, and his
directions on religious and moral questions. Even if all those
things could be contested, no critic would be justified in denying that Jesus underwent John's baptism of repentance. That
means that he was awaiting God's coming reign, and that he
believed the Baptist who said that that reign was imminent,
and had to be accepted or rejected now, at the eleventh hour.
His own preaching was in line with this; otherwise he could

have been joined neither by the 'silent in the land' nor by the Zealots, who sought by active resistance to free God's sacred land from Roman tyranny, and so died among the ruins of Jerusalem and of the fortress of Masada, which has lately been brought to light again in the new state of Israel. Two more points may be mentioned; there is no need to be exhaustive. The wording of the Lord's Prayer is not the same in Matthew as in Luke, and we may infer from this that the differing texts are liturgically edited versions of the form used in worship. But is there anything that expresses Jesus' relationship to God his Father more concisely and conclusively than these two versions, whose original form has not even been preserved? Lastly, it is indisputable that it was in his Father's name that Jesus cured those possessed by evil spirits, that he appealed to his mighty works as evidence of the dawning of God's reign, and that he therefore regarded himself as the bearer of the miracle-working Spirit.

So the problem becomes, not whether the 'liberal' man was devout, but, in so far as there ever was anything here to discuss, whether and why the devout man was 'liberal'. We do well to bring this out at once in the clearest possible way, since Jesus is not looked upon, either in the gospels or in the Christian world, simply as a representative of human and specifically Jewish piety. On the contrary, it is precisely in what we have called his 'liberal attitude' that that historian, too, regards him as being in contrast to the pious Jews of his time, and even to John the Baptist. The early Christian world brought out this contrast to the conventional type emphatically, once for all, with the messianic titles and their christology. Thus the liberal attitude of the Messiah, Christ, the Son of God, is the kernel of the problem that is raised here. It is, if we may use such an expression, a part – or even the centre? – of the christological scandal, first to the Jews, and later again and again in the history of the church. But what is true of him must also be true of his followers, and is therefore a part – or even the centre? – of the reality of salvation. Jesus' liberal attitude then becomes the authentic mark of right Christian doctrine, of true faith, of divine service on Sunday as well as in everyday life, consequently of Christian ethics, and not least, it is the object, motive, and goal of ecumenical union. By the same token, it becomes partly or mainly the limit to superstition, to questionable doctrines and practices, to unjustified church-fellowship within a particular confession and between confessions and denominations, and lastly to an ecumenicity that is conceivable organizationally and is being realized institutionally, but is at bottom profoundly un-Christian – i.e., in New Testament language, to the world-wide church of the Antichrist. We can see what is at stake. So dangerous are individual theological statements, and so little reason for surprise is there at the controversy to which they give rise. What begins as something harmless, banal, and perhaps even a trifle absurd is suddenly revealed as an explosive that may have even political effects throughout the world.

To avoid being suspected of exaggerating wildly and conjuring up phantoms, we ask still more plainly: May a church or a denomination continue to call itself Christian if its devout members have ceased to be liberal, and its liberal members can no longer be regarded as devout? Is a man a Christian if he separates two things that were inseparable in his Lord? Is it not in line with the Chalcedonian Definition, based on the New Testament and implicit in the direction in which the New Testament points, to raise these questions? It may sound secular, or even blasphemous, to seem to reduce the 'true God and true man' to the formula 'at once devout and liberal'. But is it not really blasphemous if this latter formula is not even considered, discussed, and recognized as theologically right and christologically relevant because it denies Jesus' uniqueness, sublimity, and humanity? That is what happens if the 'true God and true man' is proclaimed as an inscrutable mystery and simply accepted as true with no attempt to understand it. It is not suggested here that the Chalcedonian wording should be watered down to 'at once devout and liberal'; it is only asserted that this formula is indispensable for the right interpretation of the Chalcedonian Definition, as it specifies a crucial characteristic of Jesus, and the Chalcedonian Definition with all its doctrinal statements about the divine incarnation would be quite inadequate for a disciple of Jesus unless it found room for that crucial characteristic.

Those who were scandalized by Jesus' liberal attitude at least thought that they knew what was distasteful to God and unseemly in his Revealer, and was therefore incompatible with a Christian life and not to be embodied in the church. They had a respectable and logical theology, if nothing else. But our faith cannot rest on a theology, and therefore not on theirs, however important theology may be for the development and right understanding of faith. Our faith rests on what Adolf Schlatter, in his last little book, expressed in the question: 'Do we know Jesus?', and on nothing else, whatever the volumes of dogmatics and creeds may consider necessary. But if that is so, the problem that faces us is not merely the exact nature of Jesus' uniqueness and whether it consisted partly in the liberal attitude of his earthly life, nor is it a question about the real nature of the church; the problem is an ultimate one that goes deeper; it is in the last resort about God himself. That must make us decide who God is and who is a false god, what God did and did not do, and how he revealed himself, as being for or against our wishes and ideas about him. 'The concern with God', about which there is so much obscure or provocative talk in some quarters today, would become an overworked and misleading phrase if it did not also – or as the root of the matter – involve concern about the freedom of Jesus, and therefore necessarily and simultaneously the freedom of a Christian man and of the entire Christian community. We must add the caution, however, that this does not implicitly include what is usually termed the freedom of the churches.

So far, we have asserted that the earthly Jesus was a 'liberal', and have pointed out the christological and theological consequences of that assertion. It is now time to give it the clearcut form that is required, and to show what offence the Jews and the disciples took at it. So much has been written in the last fifteen years about the earthly Jesus that I cannot add

anything particularly fresh to it, and I content myself with
what was characteristic, instead of trying to achieve completeness. What is historically beyond question must, where necessary, be clearly noted, but not to the exclusion of everything
else. For although, even from the outset, the first Christians
were surprised and shocked at their Master's liberal attitude
and could not adopt it themselves, yet even their legendary
narratives about it reflect his uniqueness in that respect, sometimes even more clearly than the stories that are certainly
authentic. There are paintings that seize the essentials even
better than photographs, and scanty records in the form of
notes do not generally become alive till they are interpreted.
Lastly, we should keep in mind that present-day research is
trying to get beyond the point of view of form criticism, according to which the gospels have developed out of a collection
of innumerable isolated sayings and anecdotes. It is only
through this activity of collecting that we are enabled to discern the evangelists' premises and purposes, which may have
concealed the particular bearing of the scattered material at
their disposal.

On the other hand, our present point of view ought not to
make us lose sight of the theological value of what form
criticism has revealed, namely that the accounts come from a
stock of individually recorded events. The sententious and
anecdotal style favoured in the Jewish tradition indicates that
the whole gospel story was in the first place depicted in fragments. That contrasts with the present widespread superstition
that to be truly Christian one must accept *en masse* all the
facts stated in the gospels and all the statements made in the
Bible. What in fact mattered at first was simply a definite
perspective, a word that left its permanent, indelible stamp
on the whole of life and reflected Jesus himself as in a splintered
glass. The writing of the gospels begins only when the detail is
misapplied, and so needs a doctrinal framework. That again
justifies us, on occasion, in breaking off the historical process
and going back to the initial usage, so as to loosen the doctrinal
element that has grown rigid and difficult to understand readily.

So, too, a good sermon, instead of trying to say everything at once, will concentrate on one thing, possibly even at the expense of the whole. We just have to be continually learning, learning afresh, better, and more deeply; and when Jesus is concerned, we have never finished learning. Only theorists can act as though everything could be so gulped down that afterwards nothing more need happen than the belching which in some eastern countries is considered the correct thing after a meal, and shows one's gratitude for benefits enjoyed.

Some things in Jesus' liberal attitude do not go beyond what was open even to the devout Jew, or what he was allowed to do in certain difficult circumstances. In such cases authority has to decide between 'allowed' and 'forbidden', and here one school judges more leniently and another more strictly. In a way Jesus acted like a Jewish teacher, setting out what was good and what was evil, what was allowed and what was forbidden in the religious and moral sphere of everyday life. At least his community was incessantly getting him to answer questions on the subject, and to state the hypothetical and actual basic and collective rules for Jewish conduct. Think of the command about love towards God and man, or of the golden rule, to do as we would be done by. The Jews were allowed to break the Sabbath if it meant saving someone's life, and the law of purification was subject to certain specified exceptions. Because of the continual threat of defilement, and still more of being infected by false doctrine, association with Samaritans and Gentiles was unwelcome and taboo, though not completely inadmissible. Sometimes Jesus seems to have been even stricter than his opponents, or closer to the strictest Jewish practice, when, for instance, he unconditionally declared divorce and oaths to be sinful, condemned every kind of retaliation, and would not even approve of a man's sacrificing at the holy place before being reconciled to his enemy. We should not get a true picture of him if we failed to hear people who were shocked by his severity exclaim, 'Who then can be saved?'

There is certainly another side to this, again showing him taking his own line in contrast to what was generally accepted:

as far as we can see, he did not engage in Jewish casuistry; his Yes was as unequivocal as his No, and he did not waver between the two in search of a compromise. It is quite characteristic that even the earliest disciples called in the help of casuistry to correct what he had said, when it seemed to them either too strict or too magnanimous. This is shown on the one hand in the prohibition of divorce and of swearing, and on the other hand, for instance, in amplification and emphasis in the Sermon on the Mount; and it forms the basis of divergences from the same text in Matthew and Luke.

As far as all this remains within the framework of what is comprehensible and not abnormal, we need not dwell on it. Where are we to find the crucial disagreements with Judaism and with the church's scrupulosity that appeared almost immediately? In the first place, we are struck by a different relationship to the Old Testament and to the rabbinic exegetical tradition, which among the Jews itself had the binding authority of actual revelation, as the rightful interpretation of the Scriptures. This different relationship derived solely from Jesus' consciousness of a special mission, or more precisely, from the certainty that he possessed the power of the divine Spirit – a certainty that made prophetic action possible and attested the beginning of the final era in, for example, the overcoming of demons. It is true that the gospels report Jesus' consciousness of his mission, but they very rarely speak of his inspiration, although this may greatly surprise the historian, who knows that he is on safe ground here. But there is an explanation of this: just as the mere fact of inspiration seemed inadequate to those who lived later, and who laid all the stress on Jesus' being the Son of God (prophets and the Qumran community also claimed that they had the Spirit), so the Christian community very soon had unfortunate experiences with the spirit-bearers in its midst, as we shall see later. It was obviously for that reason that they were reluctant to point too insistently to Jesus as those people's prototype. Even in Qumran, where the community felt no doubt as to the bestowal of the Spirit, and expounded the Scriptures in their own special way from their own special inspiration, the words 'It was said to the men of old' referred to the laws of Moses. By transcending and correcting those words, Jesus did not simply compare himself to Moses, though even that would have been intolerable to a devout Jew. On the contrary, he put himself above Moses and the Scriptures. It is my firm opinion that that was bound to be regarded by contemporaries as blasphemy or a claim to Messiahship, and that it necessarily meant the end of the speaker's association with other devout people. The royal freedom which he displays in his treatment of the Scriptures holds good more than ever in relation to the rabbinic exegetical tradition, which is in large part simply pushed aside, as is its casuistry. The scribes may deprive their parents of what is due to them, on the pretext of having made a vow to heaven. They may in general prefer the religious to the moral duty, because obedience to God takes precedence of all earthly things. Jesus rejects such theory and practice as absurd. There is no God who ceases to be a creator, and who can therefore be played off against what has been created; there is no such thing as a God-pleasing religion that absolves us from our everyday duties; and there is no Holy Scripture that allows man to sin and relieves us of our absolute responsibility towards our neighbour. For that reason, the commandments about the Sabbath and purification are understood in a foolish way if they may be broken only in case of danger to life, and allow love to be disregarded.

It is therefore in no fanatical or high-handed way that Jesus assumes the right to be Lord of the Scriptures and Judge of religious ordinances; he does so because he judges God's word, not by the letter, but by God's will, which is not open to doubt and is not to be tampered with. The Creator claims his creation, and therefore requires our unconditional love of our neighbour and our unqualified readiness to serve and to forgive, because anything less means the ruin of every creature. Love is the fulfilling of the law. Piety that stands in the way of love stands in the way of God himself, and no theology or dogmatics has the slightest justification for arguing to the contrary. In Israel, however, the devout people and the theologians called in ques-

tion the plainness of God's will when they made themselves
the judges of what was 'allowed' and 'forbidden', using and
interpreting the Scriptures for their purpose and so binding
themselves to the letter. One may shudder in awe of an attitude
that maintains with incomparable moral earnestness that God's
commandment needs no justification, that it is enough to hear
and accept that the Holy One in Israel has spoken and decreed.
Jesus tears down even that kind of reverential barrier. God's
will is no secret, at least in so far as it concerns love and one's
brother. The creator whom one can play off against the
creature is a false god, and false gods rob even pious people
of their humanity, as is shown times without number in the
church's history. We need to keep this very firmly fixed in our
minds today. There are Christians who cry down others in the
name of a theology of the resurrection, and yet at the same
time – with certain reservations, of course – feel able to justify
the use of the atomic bomb. It sounds plausible: a bit of
genocide and world-wide destruction contrived by men is no
great matter to those who are looking only to the new world.
But with all their hope of resurrection, such Christians
blaspheme against God who, in Jesus, sought man for the purpose of helping him not merely in the next world, but here
and now. It is in this context, if anywhere, that we ought to
hear, reflect on, and preach, 'No one can serve two masters'.
We cannot serve God if we are no longer concerned for our
fellow men.

In a way, the voice of religious enlightenment comes in
here. Anyone who can evoke God out of the impenetrable
mystery, at least when it is a question of religion in relation
to morals, of worship and everyday life, of the scriptures and
love of our neighbour, is a man of enlightenment, even if he
does not suit pious people. After all, he is still bringing faith
and reason hand in hand, though they may part company
directly. Should we not honour Jesus' uniqueness in the same
terms? Is he always to remain a person who, in spite of the
cross, is to be clothed in a halo and heavenly glory, and so
turned into an icon? What is the use of acknowledging the

'true man', if in practice our acknowledgment goes no further and we allow him only a human covering? That has certainly become usual in the churches, which have always paid their respects to docetism. My faith gives me greater joy when I learn from the New Testament that even the enlightenment had some reason for honouring and claiming him, and that it connected common sense with the Holy Spirit. When the Holy Spirit is proclaimed and demonstrated in defiance of reason, it produces intolerance, hatred of one's brother and of things that are natural, illusions about heaven and earth, and a revolting caricature of the human and the divine. Whatever else Jesus may have been, he was a 'liberal'. No qualification whatever of this statement is possible, even though churches and devout people should declare it blasphemous. He was a 'liberal', because in the name of God and in the power of the Holy Spirit he interpreted and appraised Moses, the Scriptures, and dogmatics from the point of view of love, and thereby allowed devout people to remain human and even reasonable.

Anyone who maintains the 'true God' over against this liberal attitude may see that he is not sacrificing the real Jesus to an idol of his imagination and thereby destroying the basis of all Christian faith. For without this real Jesus, we do not acknowledge any faith as Christian, even if it appeals to the Trinity and the resurrection of the dead at the same time. There is still theological significance for us in the fact that the gospels could depict him as one who, in the manner of Jewish wisdom teachers, liked to use common-sense arguments; what mattered to him was agreement through understanding, not blind submission to the law. He therefore spoke plainly where today we hear so many banalities and oracles for which people presume to make the Holy Spirit responsible. The offence that he caused did not, as is sometimes foolishly suggested, consist in confronting our understanding with impenetrable mysteries; on the contrary, he testified to us of a God who does not accord with our ideas and wishes, who breaks our will and to that extent, too, any reasoning power that is influenced by our godless, idolatrous will. The free man causes offence because

he is only too intelligible, whereas the sphere of the unintelligible and the mysterious is attractive because it gives scope
for ambiguity, arbitrariness, and speculation, but not for any
real offence, and certainly not for free and happy assurance.

Having stressed our main point, we now have to pursue the
same line further. The pious people of the time were deeply
incensed by Jesus' association with sinners, tax-collectors, and
prostitutes. To understand this rightly, we have to keep in
mind the rabbinic axiom that the nation that does not know
the law is accursed. Nor should one forget that Pharisaism was
a lay movement, which tried to bring as far as possible into
everyday life the regulations for purification that were prescribed for the priests. The guiding ideal here was the priestly
nation, which through its holiness would stand continually
before God. Thus Jesus, through his associations, infringed not
only a social and political taboo, nor even simply the prevailing
moral order. He repeatedly violated what was regarded as God's
will, and in so doing seemed to attack God the Father himself.
Were not pious Jews, taken as a whole, convinced that he
really did so? Was it not indeed contrary to the preaching of
John the Baptist, so that there was now a fundamental reason
for the break that had become obvious even before Jesus began
his public ministry? Jesus, too, held to the holiness of the God
who was coming to judge the world; there is evidence of that
in the fearful curse on the places of his early ministry, and in
the relentless 'Woe' to the scribes and Pharisees, though his
action here may be portrayed only in the reflection of early
Christian prophecy.

Beyond doubt, the irreconcilable contrast with the pious
laity and theologians of his nation is authentic, for it is the
reverse side of his association with the sinners. So the cross, too,
does not become intelligible without the co-operation of the
devout Jews, even though the Romans erected it as their typical
method of capital punishment, putting Jesus between Zealots to
show that he was being executed as a messianic insurgent
against Rome. Jesus, therefore, did not disclaim the Baptist's
legacy, and it is not impossible that he likewise used hard

words about the rulers and powerful people of his time. He
was certainly not so non-political towards church and authorities that he could justifiably have been thought of as the model
citizen. For all that, the revolutionaries had their eye on him,
and felt able to set their hopes on him at least for a time. We
are now paying heavily for the fact that German Christian
people failed to appreciate this and made him a bourgeois after
their own image; and in exactly the same way his laments over
the church and the theologians of his own time have never
been taken seriously enough by those who had every occasion
to do so. His association with sinners has been mawkishly
misinterpreted, and so the terrible sternness of the judge was
glossed over – the sternness that came in order to light a con-
suming fire and bring a sword, and so revealed something of his
own inherent freedom, possibly even of rebellion. The history
of the revolutions that he has caused is not yet written, in fact
its possibility has hardly as yet been discovered, however re-
warding and well-founded such a theme might be. That shows
how constantly his reality and his impact have been effaced by
the Christian world, which incessantly fashions its own god
after its own image, and only gets furious when others do the
same or portray realistically the human nature that they
recognize.

Do we know Jesus? That is no rhetorical question, which
at once finds a satisfying answer from time to time. It is the
hidden uneasiness which keeps the history of the church in
suspense, an unfinished process which goes on from one generation to another. Of course, orthodoxy constantly tries to inter-
rupt the process, for orthodoxy is denied its claim to draw a
long breath, and it has neither humour in the face of the necessarily tentative nature of our own search for truth, nor the
essential theological perception of the fact that no one can
ever get the measure of his Lord. It takes its stand against
history and the historical spirit, without suspecting that one is
thereby opposing the creator of history. It claims revelation,
not realizing that revelation is new every day, even if it takes
the form of heretical distortions, which none the less rediscover

new country or old truth in their own, inevitably human, way.
It lives on a standard theology, even when it is carefully piling
up the miracles, in which Mr Everyman, even in enlightened
modern times, is more and more keenly interested than in
commonplace matters. In that way the church meets religious
needs that are provided for elsewhere by astrology, charms,
and yoga. The church sings, 'Thou who breakest every fetter',
but nothing is so alien to it as the One who breaks all fetters,
even devout and orthodox ones. If I may repeat it, being near
him means being near the fire, near him who has once judged
and is still judging.

It is, at any rate, characteristic of him that he reverses the
emphasis in the Baptist's preaching. He may well have begun,
'Repent, for the kingdom of heaven is at hand.' He may well
exempt no one from judgment, because he shows his Lord to
everyone. But he regards that Lord, not as the judge who will
be merciful in the exceptional case, who wants the devout to be
still more devout, who seals against the final day of wrath,
and separates by themselves, apart from the wicked world,
those who earnestly seek sanctification. For him the Lord is he
who makes the sun rise on the evil and on the good, and sends
rain on the just and on the unjust. That is the intention of the
Creator, who is continuing his work and who says to his
creatures, 'Do not be anxious', who teaches us to ask 'our
Father in heaven', and who looks to the welfare of all men by
taking their concerns into his own hands, and by grace alone
makes even devout people blessed. Because that is how the
matter stands, people are offended at him in the name of religion, and we are told, ostensibly in his name, but probably, I
think, in early Christian prophecy, 'Many will come from east
and west and sit at table with Abraham, Isaac, and Jacob in
the kingdom of heaven, while the sons of the kingdom will be
thrown into the outer darkness; there men will weep and gnash
their teeth.' Thus the history of the Old Testament is fulfilled
in a way that makes one shudder.

It is clear from this that for Jesus, the judgment is founded
on grace, on the acknowledgment of the Lord who creates out

of the void and therefore has no use for our own piety. Because salvation is there, he changes it into disaster if one does not accept it with empty hands in the carefree gratitude and happiness of a child, if one looks in jealousy, like the brother of the prodigal son, or like the earliest workers in the vineyards at a rich Father's other children who received a later call. From this, too, it is natural that Jesus calls to himself all who labour and are heavy-laden, that he does not refuse to associate with sinners, tax-collectors, and prostitutes, although the righteous, the Pharisees, scribes and Zealots also heard his voice, and in fact to some extent came to him. Jesus lived what he believed and preached, because he knew the Father and fulfilled the first commandment, first as a promise and secondly in obedience. As a judge without a peer, he would tolerate no other gods beside his Father in heaven, not even the gods of the theologians and the religious people, not even those gods of the Old Testament, wrongly imagined, and of the orthodox tradition. There is only One who merits the name of God, and that One is the Creator who 'opposes the proud, but gives grace to the humble' and awaits his lost children. He is the God who 'is our refuge and strength, a very present help in trouble', and to whom alone one can and must give his whole heart; he is the God who caused Jeremiah to prophesy, 'Cursed is the man who trusts in man and makes flesh his arm.'

That is true first of all for God's people and their piety; only afterwards might unbelievers test it and experience it. For it is the best, but also the most difficult thing in life, to have no other god but this one, the one that we cannot make after our own image. Otherwise we shall always be reckoning with the one who is fond only of devout people and therefore stands by the law, takes account of our philosophy, and appraises us by our dogmatic convictions. Otherwise, too, we shall continually be inventing one who is and remains unhuman (today people like to say 'transcendent'), although the Bible talks so much of his incarnation that it does not fight shy even of anthropomorphisms. Otherwise, again, our view of man is changed: the believer is exchanged for the accomplisher. How little it is noticed, even in the Christian world, that Jesus did not first teach his disciples to worship, but to ask (the doxology in the Matthean text of the Lord's Prayer is a later addition by the church, as the parallel Lucan text shows). For him, the attitude that man has to express is primarily that of need, which is not surpassed even by worship. Only the church sees itself united with the heavenly host in divine service; Jesus leaves man on the earth and does not call on him to transcend himself. On the other hand, it is just as important to notice that, as Adolf Schlatter was never tired of pointing out, Jesus did not tie up judgment with our short-comings; the gift received is the ground of judgment, as of salvation. Ought that not to be significant for our mutual fellowship? How much easier Christian solidarity would be if we respected in our neighbour first of all what he has received, what he has learnt for himself from the Bible and practises in his life. We, with our own knowledge, actions, and even faith, are not his standard; he is judged and blessed by what God has given him. In short: under the first commandment, God and the world and men are not as we imagine them. But we are convinced, not only that Jesus fulfilled that commandment, but that, even more, he made it seen, heard, and acted on. The first commandment, without Jesus, or indeed against him, becomes a law of death, whereas, interpreted by Jesus, it becomes the basis of human freedom and the sum of all theology and real piety, and opens one's eyes and understanding to the truth.

Just as Jesus and the first commandment go together, so the devout man and the Son of God are at the same time 'liberal'. Of course, we have to admit that this broad-mindedness is *sui generis*, and we can see this more clearly by adopting the term 'co-humanity', which in some places has suddenly acquired supreme theological importance. Did Jesus, in the last analysis, teach us co-humanity, so that we have to regard it as the essential gift and task? Still stronger than the empha-sis of this watchword is the echo of the annoyance that answers it. So it will be well to begin here, and to ask why people often bristle up when co-humanity is described as the heart of the gospel. If we are not to launch out too far into the future or the past, we might well recall Protestant history: were not the Anabaptists and the peasants who rebelled on the strength of the gospel killed off like dogs? Did not confessions lead to the waging of a war that lasted thirty years? Were not the Separatists hounded from pillar to post with the help of the police, and driven overseas? Did not Lessing have to defend himself against chief pastor Goeze in Hamburg? Were not the religious socialists ostracized by society even in our own century? Is there not an absurd quarrel over schools in countries where grown-up people live together peaceably and grammar-school education is undenominational? How does all this square with Christian discipleship and the gospel of the crucified Jesus?

There is another side to this, where it is equally necessary to ask other questions. Have churchmen and theologians never bowed before princes and magistrates, and was it not especially in Lutheranism that there developed the characteristic figure of the subject who kow-towed to the authorities and assumed what was at best a patriarchal attitude towards the proletariat? Did not my own generation grow up to be good German Nationalists or National Liberals, so that we have needed twenty years to shake off the past, bit by bit? Is there anyone, apart from a small circle, whom we can bring to realize that we no longer have anything in common with the ideals and conclusions that we took for granted when we were young? Did not our fathers ask the Almighty for a righteous victory for German arms, just as other Europeans petitioned their own national idols? Have not some of our contemporaries from the former radical Confessing Church failed to discover, even yet, that the Vietnam war is, to put it bluntly, a white man's tragedy that has finally destroyed even the artificial image of the so-called free world? Have I not with my own ears heard the European commander-in-chief of NATO say at Fontainebleau that the Christian church must strengthen the nation's defence preparations and its will to oppose the

East—as if we were still living in 1813, and as if, in case
of war, there would be anything left to defend in Germany
except scorched earth? Lastly, the bitterest recollection of our
lives: were we not, almost without exception, so paralysed
by the horror of bestiality, and so panic-stricken, that we neg-
lected to raise Cain, as we should have done at all costs instead
of leaving Jesus and the gospel in the lurch? Let others maintain
that they had known, seen, and heard nothing. Any such
excuse, which, for that matter, hardly anyone in our nation
can substantiate, would be untruthful. We were eye-witnesses
and ear-witnesses when millions of Jews suddenly disappeared
from among us, the synagogues were burnt, and urns arrived
containing the ashes of those who were supposedly unfit to
live. We were at least partly informed of these things, although we did not know the frightful scale of the atrocities
perpetrated in the concentration camps, and sometimes our
informant would ask us under his breath to keep quiet about
it. But it was a matter for all of us when tyrants and criminals
unleashed the dogs of war with no adequate reason. When
200,000 men were sacrificed to no purpose in Stalingrad, everyone had to wake up at last. It is revolting when today all this
is covered up and belittled. Of course, world history has never
been edifying; other nations, too, have a bloody past, and *homo
sapiens* has not progressed as far beyond the beast as propa-
gandists and wishful thinkers would have us believe. But anyone who backs away from his own history, however many
ghosts it may conjure up, will not profit by it or learn anything
about himself; even as a Christian he will go on swimming
in the main current, incapable of political realism, and – this
point must in no circumstances be overlooked – his faith will
be illusory.

It is true that there have always been exceptions, models of
Christian tolerance and civil courage, martyrs who for Jesus'
sake have defended people who were not thought worthy to
live, and received those who were thrust out. But does this
cover our own unforgettable shame, even though it is now
covered up and passed over in silence everywhere among our

people? Have we not shared in the blessings of citizenship, with disastrous moral results, so that Christians maintain the white man's *status quo* by watching or joining the Ku-Klux-Klan, which burns down negroes' churches, brazenly murders in broad daylight, beats women, and terrorizes large areas? The count can be continued indefinitely; it belongs to our Protestant history as does the Inquisition to the Roman Catholic. In these circumstances, how can we pluck up courage to protest, when the Bible's call to co-humanity is heard and passed on? It may not help our faith very much, but it is undoubtedly part of the gospel, of what Jesus gives, and of Christian discipleship. If that is not adequate, one can discuss the matter objectively and be assured that theology always finds its way back from extremes in its own house. Intellectual argument is part of its domestic routine, and nothing is so constant as the inconstancy of interpretation.

I do not in the least agree that the watchword 'co-humanity' represents the sum total of dogmatics and faith; but I shall recognize that throughout the world today, in view of our personal involvement in the recent past, it is a good evangelical watchword of which no one need be ashamed; it is one that we all need, and we ought to defend it unreservedly as gospel truth. I would rather be among those who have at least learnt this from Jesus and the Bible, than among the fanatics who swallow every dogma and are silent about the inhumanity tolerated and promoted by Christians, and who in their respectable orthodoxy do not first hear the voice of him who asks, 'What have you done, and not done, to me in my brother?' The sum total of dogmatics is much too difficult for all of us, and Jesus never asked anyone whether he believed in the virgin birth, the resurrection of the dead, and the descent into hell. But co-humanity is something that he actually lived, gave, and demanded. If I knew nothing else about him, I should still know about *him*. If I had no other faith to live by, I should yet live and believe with him, and one single beam of his light in our existence seems to me more important than the full sun of any orthodoxy. For according to my theology,

which I have been learning laboriously for forty years, what
is decisive for all time is not how much we have believed, but
that we have believed and followed him, however little we
have understood about him. Anyone who thinks otherwise is
welcome to count me among the heretics; in that case I appeal
to a higher court.

Now that that has been stated in the firm determination not
to correct it myself or to compromise on it, it now has to be
argued that although the watchword of co-humanity does open
out our view of Jesus, it hardly does him adequate justice. His
watchword was the reign of God. Co-humanity is the gospel's
Lebensraum, but not its basis and aim. The slogan 'co-humanity'
may be troublesome and scandalous, but it would not have
driven Jesus to the cross in his time. That was done by his
revelation of a God whom people always felt to be alien to
them (here we can readily agree with Marcion), and by his
interpretation of the first commandment against both the
usual understanding of the Old Testament and the rabbinic
tradition and the religious views of the Pharisees or Zealots. He
who went to the cross, whether consciously and of set purpose
or not – his life and message could scarcely have ended differently – is more than a prototype of co-humanity, just as he
is more than Moses and the temple. He is the ground and
object of our faith; for he is, and never ceases to become afresh,
our Lord.

What does this mean? The usual Christian answer starts
from the cross and the resurrection. That may be necessary,
in so far as it is clearly and unmistakably revealed on the
cross and to the whole world through the resurrection. On the
other hand, we are dealing at the moment with the earthly
Jesus, and it is of the utmost importance theologically that
it is he who must provide the basis of our answer. Otherwise
the cross and resurrection are brought into an isolation for
which the so-called facts can easily be made responsible. It
cannot be too strongly emphasized that the Christian faith
does not take its stand on facts that can stand in isolation. This
has become so blurred in the confessions and denominations

as to lead to widespread confusion. For we now have, on the one hand, to separate the data of faith from purely historical facts, because they are supposed to be due in a special way to God's action, and therefore to be miraculous. On the other hand, we have to guard them just as carefully from the suspicion that they are simply legends and fairy-tales; that is to say, we have to insist on their historical character. This has given rise to an unholy jumble of historicism and metaphysics, which, as it cannot be verified anywhere else, is separated from the rest of world history and called 'salvation history'. Thus faith necessarily becomes a pious acquiescence and therefore a work; and it is no use talking here about a work of the Holy Spirit. That only makes for even greater confusion. For the Holy Spirit now becomes the power that assures us of such things as we have to accept; and in that case it becomes indistinguishable, in the last resort, from the spirits of madness or stupidity, which also make us accept what there is no other ground for accepting. Anyone who invites people to have faith on the strength of such suppositions is depriving them in fact of their eyes and their common sense, as was the case with the Hellenistic doctrine of inspiration, which is not biblical, and which Paul had to oppose when he argued in I Cor. 14 against those who spoke with tongues. Man ceases to be human, even though he may claim to be inspired, if he thinks he can give up using his eyes and his common sense. That is what happens when he offers the revelation of heavenly mysteries as a substitute. Enlightened paganism in ancient times was rightly suspicious of everything that savoured of mystery, which was felt to be associated with demons and their abominations; and that suspicion is amply justified by the conduct of the Corinthians who regarded themselves as inspired. The man who is caught up into heaven loses control of himself, and is more dangerous than rationalists can ever be. For it was in the name of that god who demands blind acceptance from us that Jesus' cross was set up and every scandal of church history became possible.

This danger can be countered only if we resolutely refuse

to make salvation history a mixture of historical and supernatural facts that we have to swallow willy-nilly. We must
resist this on principle by laying it down that Christian
faith is on no account to be based on isolable data, even on the
cross and the resurrection, to say nothing of the virgin birth,
the ascension, the last judgment, the sacrosanctity of the canon
or sacraments. All that kind of thing is more or less believed
by pagans here and elsewhere, and in that way Christianity
becomes one of the varieties of human religions. In contrast
to such an approach, however widespread and dominant it may
be in all the churches, we have to declare plainly and simply :
we believe in Jesus. From this stems all else that we believe and
do not believe, and we can therefore say : we believe in Jesus
alone. That does not mean that we have nothing of the kind
to say about the creation, God's people, the cross, resurrection, ascension, and judgment, the church, canon, and sacraments. But it does mean that we may speak of all these only
as we can do so in the light of Jesus and through him. He
must not sink in the profusion of so-called saving facts, nor
even form their scaffolding. They must remain pointers to him,
or reveal themselves through him. He is neither their product
nor the code that holds them together, nor even their starting-
point or centre. In that case he would cease to be our Lord
and would become a place of wonders. They represent nothing
that could be abstracted from his relation to us and our world
and therefore be objectivized and depersonalized. They speak
of what he is doing and becoming to us, not of what he is taken
to be, and did, and becomes apart from us. Because that is so,
we cannot dispense with the earthly Jesus; he is our faith's
unmistakable *vis-à-vis*. To refer again to the Chalcedon Definition : anyone who does not confess his humanity cannot truly
confess his divinity. He may do so with events. But Jesus is no
more a mere event than he is a mere fact. He was a man,
and even then he was the Lord of his own, however much the
first disciples might lack of the final breadth and clarity that
came to them only later from the cross, from Easter, and
from Pentecost.

We have already discussed, in connection with the first commandment, how we are to regard the pre-Easter Jesus and therefore, too, the crucified and exalted Lord. Marcion was quite right in regarding Jesus as the revealer of the unknown God. He was wrong in separating that unknown God from the world and mankind, and therefore from the creation. Jesus becomes Lord by living, teaching, and bringing to fulfilment the first commandment. He reveals the God who does not fit into the pagans' ideas and metaphysics, and is even different from what John the Baptist thought. But in the light of this God the world and mankind become different, too; we can no longer see them or deal with them as we formerly did; and above all, we ourselves change from what we see in our idealism or our realism. Luther spoke of the man outside grace as the *homo in se incurvatus*, the man inescapably imprisoned and entangled in himself. He believed, on the strength of the gospel, that to see oneself so was the work of the Holy Spirit. This does not mean that that world which, according to Paul, is waiting longingly for the freedom of God's children, cannot already have some idea of it. For the Holy Spirit convinces, not from illusions, but from realities that we will not admit. He does so, too, when he lays bare to us our real sin, which is that we acquiesce in our own self-centredness, although we suffer under and complain of its consequences.

The literature of all periods is a commentary on this theme. The modern treatment of it is in part gripping and in part nauseating, as was the case in the Psalms and Job with their questions, complaints, and curses. The man who is imprisoned and entangled in himself is necessarily paralleled by the world which is in like case. How should it not express the fact in its own way? It sometimes does so, even when its writing is quite secular or atheistic, better than preachers can, because it has the art of producing something particular, and does not politely conceal the stupidity of regarding God as being away in the distance. Here, of course, the preacher of the gospel ought not to take his cue from the world by trying to outbid it in describing life's problems and guilt. In any case, we know more than is pleasant about our faults and futilities and the sin that they conceal. Jesus accepts this as a reaction to his action, but he does not provoke it. Structural analyses are not for the preacher, although the theologian cannot renounce them. Grace comes into the picture with Jesus; and the realization of sin, or the menace of judgment, is the logical consequence, not the beginning, of his actions. It discloses, not only the unknown God, but the unknown world and the unknown man; and it also interprets the first commandment, and so at the same time makes it surprisingly unknown and capable of fulfilment. For it now becomes a gift for the needy, instead of being a demand on the self-confident or the despairing. So at the end of the first part we find ourselves back at the beginning again.

We have called Jesus a 'liberal' because he broke through the piety and theology of his contemporaries, and brought God's promise and love in place of the Mosaic law, his own endowment with the Spirit in place of the Jewish tradition, clarity about God's will in place of casuistry, and grace in place of good works. He did not even hesitate to use reasoned argument and to invoke it. In doing this he was 'liberal', and no one has the right to separate devotion from a liberal approach. That shows even more clearly that he made co-humanity possible and demanded it. He did not do this on the strength of any human ideal, but connected it directly with the beginning of God's reign on earth, and he made it his aim that that newly inaugurated reign of God should be accepted and extended, that his life and death, his message and actions, should implement the first commandment; this has had the effect of giving depth and precision to the term 'liberal' when it is used theologically. He was liberal in a different way from all other people, for a liberal attitude is always a particular kind of reaction to ideals and standards that we find in our history. Jesus was indeed a 'liberal' so far as he opposed the extravagant development of the Jewish law and seemed to interpret the tradition more humanely. But that is only one aspect of his life and work, and it is not the crucial one. His attitude to the Jewish past and present was not simply a negative reaction; he broke through them with a directness that was unique. Our question at the beginning of this chapter served as an introduction to the truth that has to be grasped here, but in the last analysis it does not adequately express it. There have always been liberal people, and it is to be hoped that there always will be. He was unique in that he remained, lived and died, acted and spoke, in the freedom of being a child of God. The freedom of God's children, who were lost but are now reconciled and recalled, is his revelation, his glory, gift, and claim. Since him and through him the freedom of God's children has been the true symbol of the gospel and the final criterion for all who call themselves Christians, and also, of course, for un-Christian people who camouflage themselves with the help of church, confession, religion, and theology.

2 The Gospel of Freedom

Jewish and Gentile Christians in the Early Church; the Gospel of Mark

It is one of the many perplexing oddities of human life that we may know a thing theoretically without verifying it in a practical way or seeing through it to its logical consequences. On the other hand, we may bring to fruition some ideas that we can hardly describe precisely, and whose essential significance our minds have not grasped and formulated. So it repeatedly comes about that the theologians are often in advance of the so-called laity in perception, and the so-called laity often in advance of the theologians in practice. In this way there not uncommonly arises that schizophrenia that the New Testament calls hypocrisy. It happens time and again to all of us that we need to clarify the truth that is to be translated into action, and to translate into action the truth that has been clarified; and we cannot get rid of this kind of difficulty without mistakes and suffering, experience and hard study. Along this road we repeatedly fall back, so that we are continually having to discover old truths afresh. The history of Christian freedom is in this sense a way of suffering, on which the churches have to look back more in shame than in pride. Jesus, in his realism and his freedom, is always in advance of his Christian people, and generally in such contrast to them that they ought to talk very much more cautiously about 'being in Christ'. They must on no account do so except by asking for forgiveness as sinners and claiming the justification of the unrighteous. Anyone who has eyes can learn this, even by going no further back than the history of early Christianity as recorded in the New Testament.

We have already noticed that, although Jewish Christians put up with their Lord's liberal attitude, they did not pass it on without hesitation, vexation, and amendment. The history of his freedom involved them in continual uneasiness, sensations, and scandals – a fact that may be of some consolation to us. One of those scandals, perhaps the most momentous after the cross itself, happened only a little while after Easter. Jewish Christians set out on their way into the pagan world, a way which is still open to us, and which must indeed be taken again in changed circumstances. Few of us have any clear conception of the struggles and hardships that it cost, and with how many doctrinal problems the undertaking was charged – the collapse of the walls of Jericho seems a small miracle compared to this venture and the victory of Christian freedom. The only explicit account of it is in Acts, but unfortunately that account is by no means exhaustive or precise. It is true that Luke dwells in detail on Peter's liberation from prison by an angel, and that he devotes two long chapters, in the story of Cornelius, to the acknowledgment of the accomplished facts by the Jewish authorities. But he relates the early course of events, with striking reserve, only in a few verses, mainly Acts 11.19-26, although he feels it necessary to support his account with a number of introductory remarks, and so we can reconstruct the earlier circumstances more or less clearly.

Like the main body of Jews, the Jewish Christians who clung faithfully to the inherited tradition of the fathers did not renounce all idea of making proselytes, but neither they nor Palestinian Israel thought of a systematic mission to the Gentiles, which was ruled out by their religious beliefs. They saw in Jesus the Messiah who would restore the scattered tribes of Israel. After Easter they, or at least a large part of them, gathered in Jerusalem (which was now a very unsafe place for them) because they thought the final unification of God's people was imminent. They linked with this the prophesied pilgrimage of all the Gentile peoples, who were to witness, on Mount Zion, the triumph of Israel as the divine goal of world history. Their mission stood for the restoration of God's people,

so that he could accomplish his work on the Gentiles. It did
not enter their heads to forestall God's work, as their own
task was clear. That did not exclude the conversion of individual Gentiles, but such conversions would be only a preliminary
sign of the coming event that God had reserved for himself.

Who could blame those Christians? They had plenty on
hand if they attended to their immediate concerns and looked
after their own people. On the other hand, who can fail to
see how much our religious beliefs at any particular time
may prevent us from looking out beyond what is immediately
obvious and sharing in those miracles that we so firmly believe
to have occurred in the past? It is not a simple matter to
prepare the way for those miracles that may fall to our
lot, and to be ready to accept them. For the most part they are
contrary to our expectation, our intention, and our wishes;
and others, who seem to be most unlikely people, experience
them before us. Some of those others were in Jerusalem. They
were no less orthodox than the first group – in fact, they may
have been even more zealous. For they had come from the
Diaspora, either to settle in the holy place or to celebrate
feasts there, and so had become acquainted with Jesus and his
message. They formed a closely knit group, because they were
always to some extent strangers in Palestine, and were probably more at home with Greek than with Aramaic. They even
had their own administration in the 'seven', who were thus
sometimes in competition with the 'twelve'. In Acts 6 we
read of differences arising between the two groups, and the
care of needy widows, which was certainly an important
matter, can hardly have been the sole cause of friction.

It was not only in questions of poor relief that these Hel-
lenist disciples caused trouble. As we see in the later chapters
of Acts, they distinguished themselves by not being able to
sit still with folded hands. They were constantly going about
their Lord's business, particularly, as we should expect, among
the Diaspora Jews. The result was that the community which,
humanly speaking, would have been wise to stay quietly in
and about Jerusalem, became involved in conflicts that grew

sharper, especially as the Diaspora Jews defended just as zealously the faith that they had received, and were particularly sensitive about the Christian mission. The conflicts, which naturally increased and widened, at last boiled over dramatically in the murder of Stephen as the real ringleader. Luke (Acts 6.13) rebuts the murderers' angry charge that Stephen had blasphemed against the temple, but there may well have been a grain of truth here. Stephen had no reason whatever to decry the temple and the law, and he is hardly likely to have done so. What is quite likely is that he felt them to be overshadowed by the glory of the exalted Christ, and that he used his own version of the words ascribed to Jesus: 'Something greater than Solomon . . . greater than Jonah is here.' To devout Jews that was flagrant blasphemy, in view of the crucified Jesus.

If we accept this view, it is plain here for the first time that the church could not escape the controversy over the law, a controversy that had, in fact, begun with Jesus and later became central to Paul's theology. Its theme was opened by the Diaspora disciples after Easter and conducted exactly as in II Cor. 3. The glory of the new covenant was presented as infinitely superior to that of the old, by a spokesman who is expressly characterized as being full of the Holy Spirit, who saw as he died a vision of Christ the Son of man and Judge of the world standing at the right hand of the Father, and whose theology and piety will thus have centred on the glory of the risen Jesus.

But that is only the introductory part of the story. Luke tells us that after Stephen had been murdered, his followers could no longer remain in Jerusalem and were scattered throughout the Near East, where, however, they did not cease to missionize. Some of them preached in Antioch to the Greeks, thus going outside the Diaspora Jews. So the mission to the Gentiles began. Nothing was planned; things just turned out so – in a strange way, in fact, and one that was by no means always pleasant. Those who cannot sufficiently extol the salvation history have rarely seen it at close quarters, and so they are apt to say nothing about its attendant circumstances, which are generally most unsavoury. If the persecution in Jerusalem also affected the orthodox-minded Palestinian Jews, as Luke relates, their members promptly gathered under the leadership of the twelve. After the conversion of Paul we are expressly told in Acts 9.31 that 'the church throughout all Judea and Galilee and Samaria had peace and was built up'; so it was only the Hellenists who were so hard hit that they had to flee. Obviously the Jews were able to distinguish sharply between them and the Palestinians, and regarded the former as extremists and the latter as a harmless messianic sect of devout people. The point is that the Palestinians themselves saw things in much the same way; otherwise they would not have remained unmolested. Later, according to Gal. 2, this group, which had attached itself to James, made trouble with Peter when he fraternized with the Gentile Christians in Antioch, and it could presumably be appealed to by Paul's Jewish Christian opponents.

Thus there were already not only parties in the post-Easter community; there were also different theologies, which contrasted so strongly that the Jews recognized the fact and dealt with the groups separately. So the solidarity in suffering broke up under the stresses between those theologies. In consequence there was formed in Antioch a new centre of Christianity, and according to Acts 11.26 it was there that its adherents were first called Christians. The Gentiles gave that name to those who knew only how to preach Christ, and who did so, like Stephen, in the strength of the Holy Spirit. For them the law and the temple, to which the Palestinians continued to cling, had really passed away. Do we not see in theory as well as in practice that two different confessions, whose theology was partly traditional and partly modern, had already become separate and distinct in Jerusalem? That is not the only reason why the events are interesting.

Has it not happened in our own generation, even though it is now thirty years ago, that wrecked and 'intact' churches existed side by side, the former not being completely wrecked and the latter not completely intact, and each group seeing some representatives of the other within it? Are we no longer familiar with the fact that the main concern of one group was to maintain some semblance of order in its affairs while the other's house was on fire, and that the 'extremists' were left in the lurch by their brethren? Were not those who were jointly exposed to the terror separated by the question whether or not 'Barmen' represented a solemn declaration or a new and binding confession, and whether or not 'Dahlem', too, had consequences that extended into the organization of the church? Were not the bitterest feelings that took hold of us in those days sometimes directed, not at the Gestapo, but at the brethren – not very Christian feelings, perhaps, but entirely human? It is said that history does not repeat itself. Well, we do sometimes have experiences like those of former generations. The creation of legends very soon blurs the harshness of contrasts, so that they all get their more or less pretentious or modest share of halo. But we who are still living have not forgotten, and (it certainly is disgraceful) cannot quite get over the fact that things did not go well with Christian solidarity. Many people enrolled in the Confessing Church who later dragged their feet, favoured compromises, took part in the illusory national arbitration committees, drew in their horns when serious danger threatened, and indeed said of those whom the lightning struck that they ought not to have run such risks. We cannot forget all that, for the restoration of the German churches would never have savoured so much of reaction if there had not previously been the quarrels between parties and confessions, and if all had been willing to stand together as brothers under the same yoke and cross.

Let us at least realize that we can no longer show the same respect as before to confessions, ecclesiastical authorities, and office-holders – and to dogmatics and dogmatic theologians. That respect was destroyed when the civil courage of the individual Christian witness, or of the assembled Christian community, became the sole criterion for distinguishing between friend and foe. A little more or a little less heresy has

become a matter of indifference to us since it was borne in
on us that orthodoxy does not make the man, but that the
man very often has to put up with orthodoxy. Behind the
modern theology of 1967 the church has experienced things
which all who were involved in them would find it more than
painful to expose in detail, and which one would now rather
not investigate. The freedom of a Christian man is not given
to us ready-made at birth, and even after baptism we have
found our way to it very laboriously. If we now prove to
have become left-wing Protestant, or even revolutionary, the
responsibility does not rest with our upbringing, still less
with our desires and volition. It rests entirely with the churches
and the brethren who left us no choice, because their tradi-
tionally conservative outlook compelled them to isolate themselves from us, as the Palestinians did once from the Hellenists.
So the only way left open to us, too, has been the way to the
Gentiles, and today we sometimes get on better with the
atheists than with our co-religionists; that is a matter for regret,
but after what has been said it is understandable. Freedom
exacts its own price and has its bitter after-taste on earth, and
so we sing, 'Better in heaven, when I am with thy angels'.

If we now follow the way of the Hellenists further, we meet
with the early Christian hymns, though in the New Testament
they have survived mainly in fragments, the finest being in
Phil. 2.6 ff. and I Tim. 3.16. They all have as their central
theme the enthronement of the exalted Christ as the universal
sovereign, however much they may vary in details. In that
respect they set the pattern of the early church's christological
creed, and are already regarded by the early Christians as
specially inspired; it is here that the Holy Spirit reveals himself most directly, and the church, in its order of worship,
acclaims this with its Amen. We cannot give any detailed
analyses here if we do not want to lose sight of our theme.
What is important is that we work out the differences between
this and what the Jewish Christians of Palestine professed and
hoped for. In contrast to the gospels, the earthly Jesus is
spoken of, if at all, very mythologically, so far as his heavenly

origin and his abasement are stated. The crucial fact is that since Easter God has exalted him as Lord, and that all the powers in heaven, on earth, and in the underworld must acknowledge him as such. In that way it has come about that God, represented by Christ, rules in the midst of his enemies.

Three things are significant. First and foremost, God's reign, expected by the Palestinians, as in the Lord's Prayer, only as a future event, its existence being concealed for the moment, has actually dawned and is present. According to the introductory passage of Ephesians, the Christian community is therefore already living in the heavens, and its power already fills the earthly space wherever there is an active church that praises its Lord. The former things have passed away, and the new creation is here. The second feature in the theology and devotion expressed in these hymns is connected with the first: there is no longer an expectation, as with the Jewish Christians, of the restoration of the nation consisting of twelve tribes. Even the Jewish Christians were not, as has often been said, particularists. The re-establishment of God's people had likewise a universal horizon, because the Gentile nations were to join them in worship. But the perspective of Hellenistic Christian thought was no longer that of the Holy Land, but of the Roman Empire. Just as the poets of the imperial court proclaimed the world-wide *Pax Romana* and an altar was erected to it in Rome under Augustus, so too the Christians proclaimed, as in Eph. 2, the world-wide peaceful empire of Christ, and they set that up as the final and lasting reality, in contrast to the dreams of the Gentiles. The third characteristic of that generation follows from the first two: freedom has perhaps never in the history of the church been more passionately preached and lived than it was then. At any rate, there has hardly been any epoch in which the watchword of freedom was so generally adopted by the whole community, and in which it stood so unequivocally for the redemption and salvation that had been bestowed.

To understand that, we have to picture to ourselves the kind of world into which Christianity was born; we have accurate

information about it from ancient literature, particularly from
many papyri that have been found. The world in a broad circle
round the Mediterranean had opened out its vista, geographi-
cally, politically, and intellectually, even to the individual;
economic, cultural and religious life – all was in a state of
commotion. Christianity was only one current in the whirl-
pool, and it was quite a minor current comprising the social,
or indeed the asocial substrata, to speak in modern jargon. All
this was held together by imperial Rome with iron discipline,
and by Hellenistic civilization with internal movement and
external attractiveness. At the same time, that world was
gravely threatened, not only from its borders, but from
beneath its own foundations. Its openness was matched by its
lack of security. Demons seemed to slip out of every fox-hole,
and the power of the uncanny gripped people, even at the
highest levels. So the main question everywhere was: what
will give us stability in our changing fortune and destiny, and
protect us from the attack of earthly and unearthly powers
and from their caprices? Where is there rest for those who are
carried by dark waters to unknown shores or chasms? The
answer came from philosophers, theologians, politicians, magi-
cians, astrologers, charlatans, all proclaiming salvation in their
own way for the world as a whole, or at least for certain
individuals who were taken out of it. Redemption had to take
the form of freedom.

The young community of Gentile Christians felt the same
way; they, too, had previously regarded the universe as being
governed by the stars, and they were convinced, like other
people in the same milieu, that human beings were constantly
waylaid by demons. These Christians came mainly from the
circles most subjected to the arbitrariness of the mighty and
to the uncertain course of everyday events; and many of them
therefore had joined the mystery religions, so as to be freed
from the bonds of fate and from earthly fear. For them, Christ,
by virtue of his resurrection, whose glory one shared through
baptism, was the new mystery god. By humbling himself he
had had pity on the lowly, and now, exalted at the right hand

of the Father, he had broken through the power of the demons and stars. As Lord of all things, having conquered death and the devil, he had rendered them innocuous to those who were consecrated to him. Anyone who belonged to his expanding empire of peace had freedom now and for ever.

We shall have to offer some criticism of that preaching and piety. First, let us see where its strength lay. It answered the deepest longing of its time, and could therefore spread like a forest fire in a hot summer. The community that carried it missionized through its mere existence, even if it were not intoxicatingly full of enthusiasm and religious fervour. It gave support to the individual and meaning to the world, for it could point to the holy scriptures, which testified that the goal of history was established from the beginning, and which gave everyone his place there. We also owe to that generation the fact that the Christian world has never quite forgotten its ecumenical character, and that it has kept alive the recollection that Jesus sought out and befriended the individual. Finally, we shall have to agree that, even if we hesitate to say so after a history of two thousand years, Christianity cannot entirely do without enthusiasm. That does not simply mean that the doctrine of the Holy Spirit is an essential part of its theology, and that without the reality of that Spirit revelation and church decay. It also means that a Christianity in which there are no signs and mighty works, no visible charismata, in which the 'God is really among you' of I Cor. 14.25 is no longer heard from pagans in answer to its preaching, its actions, and its suffering, becomes empty, doctrinaire, and a form of ideology. That is a ticklish business, for of course there is always something equivocal about mighty works, charismata, conversions, and friendly or unfriendly acclamation. According to Revelation, they exist equally in the satanic realm. Anyone who is anxious to rediscover such experiences of early Christianity, or to have them at his disposal, may very quickly get from one zone into the other.

We repudiate the very widespread theological view that the Holy Spirit is something like the vital force of the transcendent

world, by its own nature kindling, illuminating, and raising
above the earth. We shall speak of this in detail later on; at the
moment we are regretting that the Christian world in general
and its representatives in particular mostly give the impression
of being so colourless, anaemic, and lacking in robustness. In-
conspicuousness is regarded as their special characteristic,
whereas resilient human vitality, personal characteristics and
intellectual independence seem out of place in them. Even with
the so-called laity, an invisible gown lends a dignity that the
wearer as such does not possess. If the Holy Spirit does not
make people more human – he very often seems to make them
unhuman! – we may doubt whether he really is holy. Christians do not hover like souls above the earth, unless they are
very quickly to become ghosts. Christian existence with no
noise going on round it is, according to Luther, not to be
thought of; and in the same way only the church that is in-
conveniently visible can become the invisible church. We have
accustomed ourselves not to show any emotions except a dis-
creet melancholy when things are sad, and a hint of rather
forced and non-committal affability when things are merry.
People feel that we are not quite of this world, but that we
try hard not to be spoil-sports; and their reaction is bound to
be the nausea that can be suitably described only in army
language. Here, too, we ought to show that repentance which,
if it is genuine, always leads us to be human. The singing of
negro congregations, which carries the attender along like a
rolling ocean, can make one forget many a bad sermon. The
communion in common, with the separate cups and wafers
given out by the elders as a matter of course in the Sunday
congregation, is nearer to the early Christian form of the
eucharist than anything in which I have taken part. Anyone
to whom preaching is not refused is also worthy of the Lord's
Supper, provided that he himself does not refuse it. For Christ
comes to the ungodly, even on Sunday morning. His coming
ends ungodliness and makes us worthy. Otherwise we are
establishing in the heart of Protestantism an utterly ungodly
and unworthy preoccupation with works.

To sum up what has been said here: early Christian enthusiasm is of the greatest theological value and of immense
practical importance for us, because we can learn from it how
the priesthood of all believers actually comes about, and ceases
to be a phrase that is often used but seldom seriously meant.
Perhaps, at any rate, we need not now go on talking about it
where that priesthood, no doubt for good reasons, is conceded
in small doses. It is not achieved by letting lawyers sit on the
church council, and letting a few members of the congregation
join in on occasion, take collections, hold Sunday school, and
look after societies and welfare organizations. This is all, at
the best, a kind of lesser clericalism, and it is a hindrance rather
than a help to universal priesthood. Of course, there are very
distressing failures where there is no longer any attempt to
attract the élite, who, in fact, cannot well be obtained with the
present methods of training pastors and teachers. But do we
not get so many failures in running the church now, that there
is no longer much left to be spoilt? Is not the worst failure in
reformed churches the congregation that has been made im-
mature except for individual representatives? Here it is worth
taking any risk. In our present circumstances, a little more
common sense all round and a stringent reduction of university
education to the really intelligent part of the population are
urgently needed. The Protestant academic élite, who today are
to a great extent using up their powers in the family, in groups
of friends, and in services of their own seeking, cannot – in
common with all economic and political specialists – be too
much encouraged, mobilized, entrusted with responsibility for
the whole or for some part of it, and called to take the initiative.
That, in our time of crisis, is more important than all the work
of administration within the church, because it is only in that
way that we can recover the chance (which has been almost
thrown away) of linking up western Christianity with the
modern world.

That is how our mission in society looks. It follows that the
parish priest is to be regarded simply as a member of a team
that he may not even direct, and that even preaching ought not

to be entirely reserved for him. Divine service must often take the most unconventional forms, and must normally, if not always, have a place for discussion – a thing that was usual, according to I Cor. 14.30-35, in the early church, and sometimes led to excesses. The congregation will have to be increasingly the outward-looking diaconate, instead of being the supposed centre of church life. If the centres of public life are no longer merely local affairs, but become regional, only the diaconate can be associated with visible boundaries. We must not object that this is revolutionary. If it should actually turn out to be so, then the Christian world needs the overthrow of old habits and ideas as much as it needs its daily bread. In point of fact, it means going back to what deserves to be called the priesthood of all believers. The basis of the frequently expressed complaint that lay people often stand aloof in emergencies is the fact that they still feel that they are in leading-strings (even though these may be long ones), and that lack of imagination, of mettle, and of thorough-going freedom produce immobility, silence, and inaction.

To give and to respect freedom is more difficult than to learn theology, although the latter cannot be entirely easy. To give and to respect freedom is, in fact, the work of the Holy Spirit, and the Holy Spirit is rarely comfortable and never without surprises; indeed, it often brings disrepute with it. No matter what danger enthusiasm may have brought to the church, the final defeat of enthusiasm has always signalized the sleeping church, even the busiest one. Enthusiasm is indispensable where the priesthood of all believers is to be awakened and the community represented and enlivened by the laity. There is no Christian freedom without a dose of enthusiasm; and today, after long abstention, that dose ought to be generous rather than meagre, even if the result should be slight intoxication. Temperance can be carried to excess, and the only way this has not been done in our country's Protestant past is in relation to alcohol. Anyone who wants freedom must give the Holy Spirit more rein than church councils and pastors have usually done, and more than they usually think suitable.

It is a real problem whether order is the last word, although the effects of disorder are not pleasant. One sometimes wonders whether a little more turbulence in our own ranks might not be good for us. Of course, any dignitary will maintain that there are already enough people shouldering the load, and that only those who cannot see behind the scenes can talk so naïvely and incautiously. That may be true; but there are also those who grieve as they sit in front of the stage and are not even given a shadow-play – a fact which, of course, annoys those concerned.

There is a Gospel which grew directly out of early Christian enthusiasm, and which – it is difficult to say whether because of that or not – was least able, in the church's history, to achieve popularity like the other Gospels. On the other hand, it is to the outstanding credit of historical criticism to have at last discovered, in the nineteenth century, that Mark's Gospel was the first to be written (although some exegetes still doubt it). It is peculiar in that it gives much less prominence than the other Gospels to Jesus' saying and proverbs, which must have come in from another source. Apart from the story of the passion, the story centres on Jesus in action. Those actions are described in exceptionally detailed stories of miracles, the most important apparently being the curing of people who were possessed. The meaning of such a presentation is clear: Jesus is the great conqueror of demons; wherever he goes, he rids the earth of them. According to 3.28ff., there is only one unforgivable sin: that of blaspheming against the Holy Spirit. That is the sin that the scribes committed when they attributed Jesus' healing power over demons to satanic gifts. On the contrary, his spiritual understanding is seen in the fact that he is the strong man who in the last days breaks into Satan's house and drives out the demons. He is therefore shown in 1.24 as 'the Holy One of God', whom the unclean spirits cannot fail to recognize as such because of their supernatural knowledge. So, according to 1.27, the witnesses of the miracle are 'all amazed', as a human being must be amazed when he is suddenly confronted with the presence of God.

Their summary reaction to the truth that has flashed on them is, 'With authority he commands even the unclean spirits, and they obey him.' We hear the same kind of exclamation by the pagans who attend a Christian service and find that they have come to a place where the divine Spirit is at work: 'God is really among you.' (I Cor. 14.25).

The earthly epiphany of the Lord of heaven is thus the central theme of Mark's Gospel. The importance of that epiphany to mankind is that it drives out the powers of evil, and so sets free the things of earth and takes them into the kingdom of God's peace. If we put it in this way, it follows at once that here the message of the early Christian hymns that Christ's accession to his dominion as Lord of all things, and of the simultaneous recognition of this by the demonic powers, was recast in narrative form and transferred to the Jesus who walked the earth. The mythical pattern of the hymns is, if one may say so, historicized. And still more, if it is part of the historically unquestionable material of the gospel recollections that Jesus actually cured people who were possessed, and that here he saw God's power at work, this introduces a complication into the making of the tradition: in the hymns, something that really took place is mythicized – expanded cosmically, in fact. What Jesus actually did is regarded in such a way as to characterize it as the saving event for the whole world. Mark himself used this proclamation by taking it out of the timelessness of a permanently valid dogmatic assertion. The dawning of God's reign was moved forward from Jesus' exaltation to his earthly life, and liturgical praise was turned into a factual account; from the hymns there survived the fact that something historically unique was of world-wide importance.

We need not here go into the question what Mark needed for his Gospel, before which there are sure to have been previous compilations such as the story of the passion, or accounts of controversies, but no real model. The keynote of his procedure is discernment; he takes various traditional items and existing collections of parts of the tradition, in such a way as to bring it all into a unity from the point of view that was preserved in the early Christian hymns. Jesus is the cosmic victor over death and the devil. He is so in the strength of the divine Spirit that fills him. He is so on earth, although in a way he is hidden because only the resurrection reveals his heavenly nature to everyone. If, therefore, God's kingdom already dawns in Jesus' coming, it is not completed till his enthronement, which is the logical end of all temporal happenings, and without which it cannot be understood in its full glory. So for the present those who know are only the demons, who have to concede that he has conquered them, and in part those who feel his power in them and who are amazed or praise him in awe. They feel that with the reign of God the empire of freedom has dawned out of earthly distress and satanic toils.

Whatever else Mark tells us about Jesus fits in with this. The fact that the power of death, which is another manifestation of satanic rule, is broken is constantly being proclaimed in healing miracles. The strength that radiates from Jesus helps the sufferers to new life, to health, to an anticipation of eternal salvation. In exactly the same way, Jesus reveals himself as the King of heaven in relation to the supposedly demonic powers of nature. Like the unclean spirits, wind and waves must obey him; for the earth is his, and all that is in it. In his hidden glory Jesus also reveals the mysteries of the kingdom of heaven in parables that he tells to his audience. Mark regards them as mysteries, because they set forth by implication and in veiled language what will be fully realized only after Christ's enthronement. Lastly, the controversies with Jesus' opponents now take on a special importance. For the upshot is always, as in 1.22, 'he taught them as one who had authority, and not as the scribes'. Here Mark anticipates what Paul lays down in Rom. 1.16, that the gospel 'is the power of God for salvation to everyone who has faith'. In his teaching, too, Jesus overcomes his enemies; and he does it in such a way as to break through the spell cast by the Mosaic law and the scribes' tradition over the will of God, and to lead men out into freedom.

Again there is no need to make a complete analysis, as that would take us too far afield. All that had to be shown was that

the first Gospel was dominated by the theme that interests us.
That is not in the least surprising, if we can get things clear.
For it is with that theme that the Gospel takes up the call to
redemption which was heard everywhere. At the same time,
it shows a fine understanding of the actual historical Jesus. His
history and Christian dogmatics support and interpret each
other here, and we can only be surprised that the exegetes have
not long since worked this out with unforgettable emphasis. Of
course, parts of the picture have always been seen, and so it
has been said that the Gospel of Mark speaks of clearing the
earth of demons. But that merely points to its mythological
background from the historical point of view, and to its
heightened christology from the theological point of view.
The expositors have not seen the crucial dogmatic perspective,
namely that Mark, unlike anyone else, wrote the gospel of
freedom. The freedom of which he spoke was not simply that
to which we are called; he also proclaimed that which was
revealed in Jesus' own physical life, and which Jesus himself
personifies beyond compare, as even the historian can still say
of him. But this freedom is such that time and again the Christian world is blinded when confronted with it; and so, during
all its history, it has kept this Gospel in the shadow of the
others, till historical criticism and religious history restored it
to its rightful place. The history of our piety, and unfortunately
even of theology, demonstrates here, there, and everywhere
that the message of the freedom of a Christian man, founded in
Jesus, has been ignored and betrayed. That involved, too, the
real Jesus and the heart of any adequate dogmatics. In this
respect the enthusiasts have protected the honour of the true
Christ and his real church against the conventional Christian
world, so that it was the heretics, or at least people with a
leaning towards heresy, who had to stand up for orthodoxy.
Against the claims of the church that mistrusted or even perse-
cuted them, they were the people who, with the inheritance
that they guarded, deserved to be called orthodox.

3 For and Against a Theology of Resurrection

I and II Corinthians

Freedom can be carried to excess. But that is putting it the wrong way: freedom can never be carried to excess; it can always be inadequately represented. But it can be misunderstood and wrongly used. That is never so clearly illustrated in the New Testament as in the Epistles to the Corinthians, which provide the classic example of Hellenistic enthusiasts. Anyone can easily see from I Corinthians what the facts were. We are not forgetting that Paul praised them rapturously: 'in every way enriched in him', 'not lacking in any spiritual gift' – that is how the letter begins. There is certainly no lack here of religious vitality; the laity are all active. It may be a little exaggerated, but it is impressive to be told approvingly in 14.26 that 'when you come together, each one has a hymn, a lesson, a revelation, a tongue, or an interpretation'. But how much is there in this very church for the apostle to take exception to that according to our ideas is right and proper? How the sins pile up, beginning with the party strife and going as far as the unseemly conduct at the Lord's Supper, from the licentious intercourse with the stepmother after the father's death (probably not directly punishable in Hellenistic law) to the denial of the resurrection of the dead. The most remarkable thing is that Paul does not make a clean sweep of it and at least excommunicate those who deny the resurrection. Sometimes, but by no means always, his praise is ironical. He recognizes

the church as such, even when he pours out his anger on it.
Obviously, things were no easier for an apostle in early Christian times than they are for a pastor today; but he did not on
that account give the church notice, carry on propaganda
against heresy, and mobilize the nucleus of devout people as
his final levy.

On the other hand, it is obviously no blessing for the Christian world if the desires of the time are too strong for it, and
the mission takes an unchecked course. In that case, the church
can never avoid accommodating itself to its environment after
the manner of Hellenistic Christianity, which regarded itself
as a variety – the highest and the true one, of course! – of the
mystery religions, and made Jesus its cultic god – the incomparable one, of course! If the church no longer has to swim
against the prevailing current, there is just as much danger
ahead as there is if it shuts itself off from its world and submits
voluntarily to becoming a religious nature preserve. It is
hard, church of Jesus, to be a Christian; one always has to fight
on two fronts, even if the centre of one's theology and devotion
it rightly defined. The question is not whether we know our
way about, but whether we turn that knowledge, however
much or little, to good account. I hear someone object that that
would mean laying the stress on the performing of works;
and of course that is possible. I only wish we would finally rid
ourselves of superstition, and allow right knowledge to be the
deciding factor. The fear of works, which sometimes seems to
be all that remains in Protestantism from the Reformation,
must not lead us to fall back on nothing but theology and idle
talk. It would certainly be better if we knew a great deal less
and lived out a modest amount of knowledge a great deal more.
After all, Jesus called disciples and did not open a school of
perfect theology or of its adepts. Grace that is not active is
illusion; only discipleship in our everyday life can justify our
dogmatics in the face of the world; otherwise we are birds
of passage in religion and philosophy, of whom there are far
too many, and where competition has long since outflanked us.

What was the reason for the unsatisfactory state of affairs

in the vigorous and highly gifted church in Corinth? Nowadays I shall be supposed to be making a feeble joke when I answer: the members were living on a theology of resurrection, which they regarded as decisive and which was the only one that they allowed themselves to digest. Yet that is the proper, necessary, and very helpful answer to the question asked. I might equally well have said: they lived on a misunderstood theology of freedom. For these two go together. At the same time one must realize that a misunderstanding of freedom arose from a theology of resurrection. We have seen that Hellenistic enthusiasm was centred in faith in the exalted Christ as the Lord of all things. Those Christians were convinced of his lordship, and they extended it by virtue of the Spirit with signs and wonders, with dealings in mysteries, and with inspired utterances of wisdom. The exalted Lord manifested himself mightily in them, and through them to the world. But he had been exalted since his resurrection; and that was so important to the Corinthian church that it set no great store by the earthly Jesus. According to I Cor. 12.3 there could even be heard in its midst the ecstatic cry, 'Jesus be cursed', meaning the earthly Jesus. When this was matched by the equally ecstatic cry, 'Jesus is Lord', the reference was to the exalted Lord after his resurrection. At bottom, even Jesus as Lord did not matter a great deal to the church, at least to its enthusiastic majority. The main importance that his resurrection and exaltation had for them was that they showed that the new world had begun. Theologians would say that in a twinkling these people changed christology into soteriology, and so came back very quickly from Jesus to themselves, namely to the salvation that he had mediated to them by being, as it were, simply the ignition for the fulfilment of their own longings. Thus they showed that, even as a Christian community, they were less representative of characteristic discipleship than of the prevailing hopes and desires for salvation in their environment.

But in what way could his exaltation and their assurance of salvation be combined? After all, one cannot simply appropriate to oneself something that happened to the Lord. This

brings us to the paramount importance that the sacraments had
for the Corinthians. The disorder at eucharistic celebrations
did not come about through any lack of regard for the eucharist
in the setting of a love-feast; on the contrary, the Lord's Supper
was celebrated as an anticipation of the heavenly banquet
amid eschatological rejoicing and ecstatic manifestations such
as, perhaps, speaking in tongues. It was a demonstration of
what was taught in Eph. 1. This church knew itself to be
already redeemed 'in the heavenly places', filled with divine
powers, open to the permanent invasion of the earthly by the
eternal, and itself testifying to this through its behaviour. The
same is true of baptism, which, as we know from 1.10ff., was
made an occasion of party divisions. For the baptized people
split into different groups according to the master who had
baptized them or by whose name a particular group was de-
signated. The members were supposed to be joined to him by
supernatural ties, as is maintained in the church's history
wherever the baptizer and the baptized may not marry each
other.

It is on this basis that we may answer the question that is
suggested by the point of view put forward in I Cor. 15. It
seems as if the Corinthian enthusiasts had denied Jesus' resurrection and any rising from the dead, both for themselves and
for others. In fact, Paul himself seems to have understood it so,
as he learnt of the dangers in the community only through
messengers, and could not get a completely accurate picture.
We are inclined to suppose that behind the denial of resurrection there was an enlightened philosophy which already existed
in certain upper strata of Hellenism. But that means that we
are transferring to early Christianity the picture of present
conditions; for in Corinth there were virtually no representatives of the upper stratum. The church was composed almost
exclusively of the waterfront proletariat of the town which,
as well as being a centre of world trade, was famous throughout
the Roman empire for its innumerable temples, and notorious
for its proverbial immorality. It had for its background every
kind of superstition, magic, and mystery cult, but not by any

means enlightenment. Of course, even in that church, Jesus' resurrection was not doubted. Apart from the fact that in that case one could hardly be called a Christian, as the message of Jesus' resurrection and exaltation provided the central message for the Hellenistic world (see I Cor. 15.3ff.!), the course of affairs in Corinth makes it clear that people lived on the assumption of the invasion of the earthly world by the heavenly. That is why they valued speaking in tongues as the language of the angels and of the world beyond. They attached no importance to the future raising of the dead, though this did not come from a kind of rationalization, but because they acknowledged, with Eph. 2.6 (probably a fragment of a hymn), that God has raised us with Christ 'and made us to sit with him in the heavenly places'. The same is expressed in Col. 2.12f. and elsewhere in the New Testament, as the Johannine Christ bestows on his own people resurrection and eternal life, even in the present.

According to Hellenistic ideas, this takes place at baptism, which mediates the power of the supernatural by granting us the Holy Spirit, and, according to Col. 1.13, 'has delivered us from the kingdom of darkness and transferred us to the kingdom of his beloved Son'. That is put so realistically that death is no longer feared. In death men simply cast off the outer covering that hides the new, heavenly, spiritual body. Death frees us from the last ties attaching us to the old world, but makes no other change in our new existence. We may again quote John, who says of the believer, 'He does not come into judgment, but has passed from death to life.' We are not now concerned with what John understood by this, but only with the wording, which expresses most realistically the ordinary view of the Hellenistic Christian enthusiast, namely that the baptized person already belongs to the heavenly world. In truth he has already risen with his Lord, and has therefore become like him in exaltation as in death; he shares in his lordship over all earthly things, because he shares in his victory over the demons and over sin, death, and the devil. As this was what the Corinthians lived, believed, and proclaimed, they would have nothing to do with any future raising of the dead. They were convinced that what was held out to them as something for the future had already come about, and had become, here and now, salvation, the new creation, and eternal life, which had begun in baptism, and were to be confirmed and demonstrated at the Lord's Supper and in daily life.

The connection of a Christian cult, analogous to the mystery cults, with a resurrection theology oriented on man is evident, and uncommonly instructive for our own circumstances. For we cannot shut our eyes to the fact that even in Protestantism we can observe a so-called sacramental realism, stressing the objective realization of heavenly forces in the cult, and apparently advancing irresistibly. Hand in hand with this goes the devaluation of a theology of the word, of faith, and of the cross. It is at once comprehensible and grotesque that here the conflict with supposedly modern theology finds strong support. It just goes to prove that the 'modern theologians' are representatives of the Reformation, whereas the pretended realists represent the enthusiasts in the wake of Christianity.

We can now understand all the circumstances that strike us as peculiar in the Corinthian church. Anyone who feels himself to be a citizen of heaven and permeated with heavenly strength no longer needs to take the earth seriously. He has all the less need to do so if he has already been drawn into the largely orgiastic doings of the mystery religions, and is accustomed in his proletarian existence to accident and uncertainty, so that one must not assume that his old Adam is strictly regulated. Exuberant religious vitality breaks through every dyke and stops for no bourgeois taboo. Thus, at any rate, the problem of the emancipation of slaves and women appears on the horizon, although not in its modern version. The call of Gal. 3.28 chimes in with baptism: 'There is neither Jew nor Greek, there is neither slave nor free, there is neither male nor female; for you are all one in Christ Jesus.' As some such formula appears several times in the Pauline letters, we may assume that it represents an established tradition of the Hellenistic church that was quoted by the apostle. In Corinth, the formula was evidently not intended to be merely edifying and spiritual. Anyone who is translated into the heavenly sphere claims equality at least with the Christian brother, the Christian spouse, the Christian master, first in the congregation assembled for divine service and then in everyday life. Why should the woman keep silence when the Spirit has come upon her? Why should the slave consent to be dependent on a Christian master? Why should not prophets and those who speak in tongues speak as often as they wish, if they are inspired? Why should one not on the one hand practise asceticism to show that his state is like that of the angels, and on the other hand cohabit with his stepmother to show that Christ has freed us from the moral prejudices of a bourgeois world? Freedom has become the real and the sole mark of the Christian and the church. Do we not renounce all the bliss that has been bestowed on us, if we do not turn it to account incessantly and in relation to everyone?

I hope it is now clear that in Corinth a consistent theology of resurrection led to an equally consistent theology and practice of freedom. It must be evident, too, that the Corinthians were not deeply and permanently interested in christology. That is true, although the doctrine of the exalted Christ who rules the world, and in whom they have achieved a share that is constantly renewed in the sacraments, is the basis of their theology and practice, so that without it everything would collapse. But they listened to nothing in the proclamation of Christ's lordship, except in reference to what he gave to his own people. In reality, he became the agent and the implement of grace, like the coal-carrier who unloads his sack of fuel at our back-door. As Lord of the individual life, as Judge of our conduct, as the Exalted One whom we have to serve, he no longer counted. That means, however, that what now really counted was not Jesus Christ himself, but only his gift, so that the main emphasis was on soteriology and therefore also on religious anthropology. As to how salvation affected one personally after it had been received, what is most apparent is that it obscured the glory of Christ.

We have had to go into these matters in detail, so as to grasp the difficulty of the apostle's situation. His most dangerous opponents in Corinth were perhaps not the Christians who, in denying the resurrection of the dead, had fallen back into pagan unbelief and the pagan confusion associated with it. More dangerous than these were the fanatics for whom God's kingdom had already begun on earth, and who wanted to demonstrate it in their own bodies and in their lives and their behaviour. It was not Paul's main concern to remind them of the resurrection, for what he found was a theory and practice of the reality of resurrection which he himself, in I Cor. 15 (written on the basis of the information that he had had), did not entirely fathom. That theory and practice may have been developed from his own preaching, or more probably from that of gifted missionaries, such as Apollos, who were more nearly of the enthusiastic type. In any case, the development was analogous to the mystery religions' preaching of the dying god restored to life, who brings along a new world in which his own people are to share. Strangely enough, therefore, the apostle had to take up a position – in a Christian church, of all places – opposing a theology of resurrection. How he managed to deal with it is an intriguing question; for he could not deny Jesus' resurrection, or God's sovereignty which it inaugurated, or the reality of Christian freedom, without betraying both his own preaching and the gospel itself.

There are three things that characterize his position, and they necessarily interlock and complement each other. But it is important that we begin with the crucial one, which is that we do not hear the apostle preaching first from his opponents' stronghold – from soteriology and anthropology. Here, too, of course, he will have to make assertions that distinguish him from his opponents. He will therefore have to describe the essence of Christian faith as obedience, as hope, as love; and thus he will set bounds to the arbitrariness of the enthusiasts. But he can do this only if he, for his part, bases that essence on a christology that is basically different from that of his opponents. This he does at once at the beginning of the letter, by characterizing the gospel as 'the word of the cross'. For him, too, Christ is the Risen and Exalted One, who was ordained by the Father to be Lord of all things. But for all that, for Paul he remains the Crucified One. That is not meant historically, so that the cross is the way to exaltation, although that naturally was the case. It is meant, rather, that Christ, exalted above the cross in his sublimity, is misunderstood if one separates the exaltation from the cross, and so reduces their relationship to that of two merely consecutive events. The Risen and Exalted One remains the Crucified One; and his sovereignty is not understood and acknowledged if the cross is merely made the last station on his earthly way, as, in fact, is done by the enthusiasts. 'Risen so as to be Lord' means 'Risen so that the cross may conquer the world'. There are plenty of risen gods in the history of religion, especially in the sphere of Hellenism; and there, too, the way is by a journey through hell. If the cross is simply the gloomy entrance to heaven, the final and the utmost obstacle to triumph, the Christian message does not fundamentally differ from what can be said by competing religions.

Unfortunately, that is very often the case. It ought to disquiet us when Christianity has nothing more to offer here than the fulfilment of pious or carnal longings for the conquest of the grave. If Christ is only the model on which we set our hopes, everything is spoilt, and we had better take to anthroposophy. Other people have other models, in support of which they can bring their own evidence. It is here that there must be shown what, in fact, the average funeral sermon fails to point out, that our God helps against our will and our wishes, never without vexation, but always in such a way as to honour the third petition of the Lord's Prayer. The only distinctive mark that completely separates Christianity from other religions and their gods is the cross, although we shall later have to consider the fact that imperial Rome set up many crosses. By characterizing the gospel as 'the word of the cross', and by declaring that he had 'decided to know nothing among you except Jesus Christ and him crucified' (I Cor. 2.2), Paul emphasizes that the core of his doctrine of resurrection remains the cross. The point is that the resurrection is one aspect of the message of the cross, not that the cross is simply one chapter in a book of resurrection dogmatics. According to Phil. 2.9, God has exalted only the crucified Lord, whose kingdom, sovereignty, and triumph are God's kingdom of resurrection.

It is no accident that there is yet another passage where the apostle contradicts his opponents' christology. They call Jesus the Lord of all things, as the New Testament hymns consistently do. One is bound to regard it as a criticism of that expression when, in I Cor. 15.25-28, although Paul has 'Christ must reign' as the central theme of his doctrine of resurrection, he at once adds the qualification that death remains the last enemy and has not, for the present, been overcome. He does not think that Jesus' assumption of sovereignty means the end of history, although it does mean the end of the law. Even the exalted Christ is not the last word; his sovereignty is still being disputed by the power of death, and is therefore contested till the end of time, and is therefore questionable. We can call him the Lord of all things only in faith and in the light of his or- dained destiny; for the present he is only the Lord of his church, and then, of course, because the church is continually penetrating into the world, he also claims sovereignty over the world. If one may exaggerate somewhat, he is still in the ranks of the fighters. In any case, he is not yet the final victor, for that would presuppose his undisputed lordship over the world. For Paul the exalted Christ still bears the nail-marks of the earthly Jesus, but for which he would not be identical with Jesus.

The Reformation has indicated the facts of the case so plainly that no discussion here ought to be necessary. Strangely enough, however, the Reformation churches are no longer able to handle it with that clarity that their confession requires. The Re- formation aimed at pursuing a theology of the cross in con- trast to a theology of glory. Today such antithesis and polemics are almost completely forgotten. The cross is understood in a devotional sense, for example as a pattern of our own destiny;

and then, of course, the reality of the resurrection has to be the conquest and the end of the way of the cross. The two are separated from each other in contrast, as in the saying 'Through the cross to the crown!'. We shall have to consider later the fact that it was used even in early Christian times; it certainly does not come from Paul.

On the other hand, the two are put alongside each other, because it is a matter of the links of a chain or the rungs of a ladder, the resurrection always being regarded as the last, the highest, the final goal. That may be justified in view of the end of world history. But we have not yet reached the end of world history, and so we cannot speak of the present time as triumphantly and precisely as the enthusiasts do. If we are to remain in the reformed tradition, the reformers' view of the theology of the cross as antithetic to the theology of glory must in all circumstances be continued today in the antithesis of the theology of the cross to a definite and even dominating theology of resurrection. Wherever the resurrection message obscures or restricts, even in the least degree, the message of the cross, the resurrection is not rightly taught, either in the Pauline or in the reformers' sense. In that case, Lutherans, even in high places that they have inherited, will no longer be rightly called Lutherans, and those of the reformed faith, even in theocracies, will no longer be rightly called reformed according to God's word. That is where the enthusiasm predominates, against which Paul had to take the field in I Corinthians. There today's true *status confessionis* is given, the point at which one must stand one's ground and fight it out at all costs. That is where genuine orthodoxy that is worthy of its name parts from imaginary orthodoxy, just as wrongly so-called heresy parts from actual heresy. Pious turns of speech mean absolutely nothing here, and at present can only make one suspicious.

The apostle corrects not only the enthusiasts' christology, but also the doctrine of salvation that proceeds from it. We can see this plainly when he reminds the Corinthians that at the Lord's Supper a share in the crucified Jesus is given and his death is proclaimed. In the same way, he says in Rom. 6.2ff.

that in baptism we do indeed die with Jesus, and receive only
the pledge of being raised again in the future. I Cor. 10.1-12 is
directed polemically against the enthusiasts' general understanding of the sacraments: baptism and the Lord's Supper do
not guarantee salvation, but put us on the way of the new
obedience, and thus, indeed, into a position of temptation and
trial, which can cause us to fall like the people of old in the
desert. Thus water is poured into the enthusiasts' wine; they,
who fancy themselves already in heaven, are brought down to
earth; that is what must happen when the Crucified One is
preached as Lord. Salvation is certainly in his sovereignty, but
that sovereignty first of all demands our service. There is no
sense in talking about Christ's lordship if even Christians are
not willing to recognize him as Lord in their conduct. Just as
the sacraments give them a share in Jesus' death and bring
them hope, so the Christian everyday routine calls them to
love.

Love, however, as was the case with Jesus, includes the use
of reason. No one can love who shows no consideration to his
brother, or who stifles his own conscience; nor can anyone love
whose sole concern is his own personal prestige and who pushes
his own gift into the limelight, as those who speak in tongues
do. Lastly, no one can love who quarrels, goes to law with
his fellow church member, and gives the world occasion for
scorn or moral offence, as incestuous people do. Never do we
have salvation in ourselves. God has made Christ our wisdom,
our righteousness and sanctification and redemption (I Cor.
1.30). He alone is our salvation, which consists in nothing else
than having him as Lord.

From this we may draw conclusions about Pauline anthropology. The apostle expressly emphasizes, quite in line with
the ideas of early Christianity as a whole, that baptism imparts
the Spirit, and that Christians are bearers of the Spirit. We are
told categorically in Rom. 8.9: 'Any one who does not have
the Spirit of Christ does not belong to him.' Paul also recognized and extolled, as no other New Testament writer, the
multiplicity of spiritual gifts. He called on everyone to find

out his own particular gift and abide by it, so as to be fruitful in good works and helpful in building up the body of Christ. No one can serve unless he will go into action with his own distinctive contribution; what everyone can do is only boring if there is another Christian doing it. As there has to be a place in the church for all special qualities, everyone has to activate his own particular gift. The buried talent makes us liable to judgment; that ought to be borne in mind and preached today, when talents in the Christian church are for the most part buried, and the office-bearers only too often help, consciously or unconsciously, to dig graves for them. Other people, on the other hand, presumptuously imagine that they have gifts – theological capacity, for instance – which have been denied to them, because catch-phrases and a liking for the sound of one's own voice are not enough. Discriminating between different spirits (an unworked field, in spite of all the heretical propaganda) includes recognizing what I am not suited for. If anyone should fail to see this in his own case (we are all of us the least able to see ourselves), he should be called to order, kindly, but promptly and clearly. It is true that the Spirit opens the heart, but sometimes it also stops the mouth.

If that is so, it is clear that Paul admits the Spirit as a heavenly gift only so far as he exercises responsibility regarding it. Ecstasy will not do it alone, no spiritual gift will do it alone, since they are all, in an earthly context, only fragments. Indeed, in I Cor. 14 Paul goes so far as to lay down regulations for inspired persons, and restrain the spirit that is at work in them. What does that mean but that even the bearer of the Spirit has to remain under the cross of Christ? We cannot share in Christ's glory except by bearing his cross after him on earth. The apostle repeatedly reminds his churches of this in the example of his own life, giving a long list of his sufferings. In view of Gal. 6.17 one might be bold enough to assert that Paul recognized no bearer of the Spirit who did not bear on his body the marks of the Lord Jesus, although the apostle was referring to some special marks here. Christian existence thrives only under the cross. If it breaks away from that place, even by a very little, if it is wearing a halo that keeps the shadow from being seen, then that life is not Christian. The theology of resurrection as the enthusiasts represent it is pursued by the apostle into its last hiding-place and cleared out, always under the same banner and with the same authority of the crucified Christ. We can remain under the power of the resurrection and in the real hope of being ourselves raised again, only when the crucified Christ rules over us and is glorified through us.

How do things stand, then, with Christian freedom? It seems as if I had spoken only of service, responsibility, sufferings, of discipleship. My critics are sure to take me up again here and maintain that the theology of the cross, which I have defended and played off against the enthusiasts' theology of resurrection, is really a variation of the law, namely its Christian modification. I am afraid they will not cease to do so, although in the previous chapter I so stressed the rightness of and the need for enthusiasm in the church that even my severest critics in the Protestant camp cannot deny my courage, and perhaps even my rashness. Theology is not such a simple matter that we can talk about the law when we ourselves and others are expected to do and suffer something. The whole New Testament demands of us so much so uncompromisingly that it takes our breath away. Is all that nothing but law? Are we schizophrenically to separate the two, the gospel and the law, till they keep on changing round so that no one knows whether the New Testament is determined by the gospel or by the law? The demand does not yet make the law, just as the preaching of salvation does not yet need to be the gospel. For there are false prophets who cry salvation when disaster approaches of which they ought to give warning. Today the stock-in-trade is clichés, which correspond to the technical society's mass consumption, but which hinder the thought, independent judgment, and real instruction of others.

According to Paul, the law operates by fear; but the gospel drives away fear and leads us to cry, Abba, dear Father. In other words, it takes us into the freedom of God's children. Just as the attack on the Corinthians' theology of resurrection does not deny the resurrection but understands it differently, so the theology of the cross does not get in the way of the freedom of God's children. On the contrary, it is the only thing that puts it where it should be, between blind obedience and the enthusiasts' excesses. Paul was at least as open-minded as anyone in the New Testament towards the theology of freedom and the enthusiasm of his environment. He had unreservedly adopted Jesus' message and methods. But the message of freedom that he preached led to different conclusions from those of the enthusiasts on the resurrection. On an exegetical basis, but putting it very summarily, we may say that he felt freedom to be, not the logical outcome of a resurrection that had already taken place, but the anticipation of a resurrection that was expected. Jesus' resurrection is bestowed on us for this present time in baptism, in the gift of the Holy Spirit, and in Christian everyday life, but not in such a way that we are sharing in his resurrection as well as in his death and are given a heavenly instead of an earthly nature. What it does is to give us a share in Jesus' death, to let us bear the cross after him, and to set us, for the first time, firmly on the earth. According to Phil. 3.10, the result of knowing him and the power of his resurrection is that I 'may share in his sufferings, becoming like him in his death'. We should notice the wording. The apostle does not talk about my simply having to take up my own cross, although that, of course, is part of the matter. He talks about sharing his sufferings and being in growing conformity with his death. That is in line with his sacramental teaching and with the sense of the various Pauline catalogues of sufferings, which are regarded as being in Christ's service, and therefore as emphasizing the shadow of the cross.

People who, like the Corinthian enthusiasts, are never tired of stressing the present power of the resurrection, at once resort to subtleties when the question of one's involvement in the cross is raised. Has this question been confined to discussions by mystics and exponents of the law? I entirely agree with them that the Lord's cross does not merge in ours or merely provide a model for it, but is faith's basis and ideal – exemplar,

not example, says Luther! But according to II Cor. 13.4, Jesus'
cross, after he himself had been exalted, remained present on
earth in such a way that we, representing him, bear it after
him. We must not fall into the error of the enthusiasts, who,
for the sake of the risen Lord's presence, turn the cross into a
historical affair. That must not be done, even if it is described
as a unique supreme sacrifice and a once-for-all reconciliation.
Jesus' cross has not passed away on earth; it is now borne, not
by him but by us as his delegates. It is not a saving event of a
kind that can be isolated, as a historical event that has occurred
only once can be isolated. Jesus' cross remains set up on earth
as a sign of divine truth and of the offence that it causes to
the world. The God of the cross is our only God; but he is the
God whom the world can never accept unless it has been converted. Anyone who limits the significance of the cross for
Christianity and the world obscures God's truth and the offence
that attaches to grace. He inevitably falls into the realm of
superstition, even if he is supporting a theology of resurrection.

In this connection we ought to remember again, and seriously, that Paul wrote to the Corinthians critically, not only
about the cross, but also about the last judgment. It is a strange
state of affairs that in our day his remarks on the latter subject
have been taken up summarily in defence of future eschatology,
in contrast to a so-called modern theology. But they are hardly
ever found where they would be most of all appropriate in
our own circumstances. It cannot be disputed – most funeral
sermons testify to it with distressing plainness! – that the hope
of overcoming the grave provides the most solid bulwark of
the theology of resurrection that is proclaimed so loudly. Here
is centred the interest of the devout community that is dis-
quieted by modern theology. How its numbers would diminish,
or at least how its enthusiasm would wane, were it remorse-
lessly stated on every coffin: 'We must all appear before the
judgment seat of Christ, so that each one may receive good or
evil, according to what he has done in the body' (II Cor. 5.10).
That was addressed primarily, not to the world, but to devout
people, and it shows that in Paul's view the last word was not

with our survival, but with the glory of Jesus.

Even the making present of heavenly powers in the cult does not protect anyone from the judge; it rather exposes him. One does not necessarily gain anything by simply being raised from the grave. For the apostle that is only the beginning. But if death and resurrection mean that we have to appear before our judge, it becomes clear why the theology of the cross also remains the centre of the Pauline preaching of the resurrection: what ultimately matters is not that we genuinely believe and defend this preaching, but that we accept it as a call to walk as Jesus' disciples and to share in his death. Everything else is nothing but the widespread religious expectation of a life of bliss, an expectation with which nothing that is specifically Christian has, as yet, had any contact. Indeed, if we may put it so forcibly, in our time the normal dominating urge of a bourgeoisie is to maintain the *status quo* in all circumstances and to survive, the purpose of religion being to ensure this in the face of death. How much easier a theological understanding would be between groups that are today opposing each other, if we could at least agree that we cannot and do not want to defend bourgeois transcendence in the name of Jesus. Formerly it may have been a point of contact and a support for our message. Today it serves to falsify that message, however badly any attempted revival is hampered by our churches' small-minded involvements. It is only from the cross of Jesus that we can recover the necessary freedom of movement in life and thought. It really is tragic that a theology of resurrection limits that freedom and promotes reaction in all spheres.

The point of all that we have said is that in the school of Jesus we learn to say sincerely 'Yes' to the cross, and, however incredible it may sound, to bear it willingly. As the world hates and fears the cross, so Christians come to have an affection for it. There is no need to be so extravagant as to suppose that Christians must always and everywhere strive for martyrdom and mortify themselves as the ascetics do. Nor should they indulge in that disagreeable melancholy that bewails and condemns the state of the world even by one's facial expression.

Lastly, it would be wrong to suppose that Christians learn
in a moment to suffer willingly, and that they no longer sigh
like Job when they have trouble with Jesus' and their own
cross. It is true that we are often assured that death is easier
for Christians than for pagans. I have never been able to con-
firm that, although I have stood at hundreds of death-beds.
There are pagans who die laughingly, and Christians whom
death dismays, and, of course, the reverse is also true. A man
counts as a lover of the cross only in so far as it enables him
to come to terms rather with himself and others, and with the
powers and enticements of the world. Under the cross man
attains manhood, because that is where God reveals himself
as what he really is – our Creator. As our Creator, God is for
us and claims us as his creatures; that is the truth and the proof
of love (Rom. 8.31ff.). Under the cross of Jesus we experience,
with the Lord Immanuel, God's love which stoops to the lowly,
and at the same time we learn in consequence to live from that
love, which triumphs over good and evil: Abba, dear Father.

But to live from that love means to stand in the freedom of a
Christian man. Anyone who is sustained by love is taken, in
the same way, out of the reach of fear and pride. He no longer
needs to be anxious for himself, or to worry about the lures
and threats that intrude on him. He can hold, because he is
held. On the other hand, he cannot boast, and what he himself
has and is becomes unimportant, because he must be held. To
live from the Spirit does not, as the enthusiasts suppose, mean
being something that has to be shown off for one's own sake.
It means to live from grace as a created being, to live from the
other, who is our Master. So this state in God's love becomes
essentially a state of obedience. Nothing is more demanding
than love; it wants us wholly and for itself alone, so that in it
the first commandment is fulfilled. Obedience means first that
we learn to hear again and again, and always anew, 'I am the
Lord your God'. But one cannot hear that without at the same
time hearing the call of the jealous God who allows his creature
and his honour to no one else: 'You shall have no other gods
besides me'. That is our sanctification, that we belong to one

God and to no one else. We are concerned with many things, and we are so constantly meeting the gods of this world, namely whatever the world has nearest to its heart, and whatever it trusts in the hour of need. Paul shared the view of his time that the decisive factor in the world is its gods. For him, therefore, a man's manhood does not begin till he can meet those gods defiantly and without embarrassment, since at bottom they no longer concern him. They are a reality, but no longer his life's truth, which is given in his Lord. All the actions and sufferings of the Christian, therefore, amount in the last resort to one thing: no longer to fear and love the other gods. The disciple's whole being stands or falls in the fight against idols, a fight which may leave him sometimes calm and amiably cool, sometimes angry and scornful, now on top, and then again suffering and dying. The Christian is forbidden to give his heart unconditionally to any thing or any person.

This is true of our attitude to ourselves even more than of our attitude to all other powers. The other gods are in fact always the objectivations of our longings and fears, our pleasures and our wantonness. They are born in our hearts, and then, from the man who creates them, they gain power over him and over the earth. What influences our hearts always makes itself felt outside, acquires influence over our surroundings, and finally enslaves us and others, so that it comes at us again from outside. Thus the world's great forces of evil arise from human illusions which we cannot shake off, and which grow stronger than we, our society, and the efforts of the nations. For this reason, Christ's victory begins in our hearts. That does not eliminate the evil forces that surround us; but if the spell is broken in one heart, the good effects spread indefinitely. The church that is worthy of the name is the band of people in which the love of God has broken the spell of demons and strange gods and is now pushing its way into the world. Where there is a real church, the world is, within a larger or smaller radius, cleared of demons, and God's sovereignty over his creatures begins in a new way. But it begins in no other way than in individual hearts, though it does not

end there, any more than the demons do. It, too, wants not
souls only, but the world, because otherwise God would not
be God. It even creates institutions, because without institutions
man cannot live, even as a partisan. It can express itself, too,
in religious denominations, because God has not made us all
to the same pattern, and can only help dissimilar things and
people to complement each other.

Finally, God's sovereignty strives for ecumenical unity, because the Lord remains the same over the many and the diverse.
German Protestantism desperately needs to wake up at last
from the stuffy provincialism to which it became addicted
when it surrendered, first to the protection of the provincial
rulers, and then to the inward passivity of idealism. Now we
do not even know about the innumerable other churches and
denominations, to say nothing of any concern for the social
and political problems that are not in the shadow of our own
church towers. The enthusiasm that breaks through such bar-
riers is to be praised; but that does not alter the fact that everyone has to begin with himself, give his heart entirely to God,
and take it away from the gods. Everyone has to sweep before
his own door, and in daily penitence, in the dying of the old
Adam in himself, to become a new creation. Paul describes this
with the words, 'It is no longer I who live, but Christ who lives
in me'. That is the first commandment, applied to the disciple;
and it means nothing else than the Johannine 'He must increase, but I must decrease'. If we want to invoke the law,
we may do so only in the sense in which Rom. 8.2 speaks of
'the law of the Spirit of life in Christ Jesus'. For it is the law
of love, by which I belong to him who has given himself to me,
and the law of sonship, by which the Father's will is done in
the Father's house, and the law of freedom, of which Paul
says in I Cor. 3.22f., 'All are yours, and you are Christ's'.

The enthusiasts are quite right to have noted 'All are yours'.
For the sake of the cross, on which Christ gave himself to us
and in whose love we can and are to overcome, the Christian
walks through a world freed from demons. He no longer has
any taboos, even in a theology which demythologizes and

which illuminates the canon by radically historical criticism. If we are no longer afraid of angels and demons, we certainly ought not to be afraid, either of reason in its ardent quest for a more accurate view of the past, or even less of nature as it reveals its secrets. It is right and proper for us, as genuinely inquiring human beings, to concern ourselves with what has happened and is happening; and there is no need to blindfold ourselves, as many feel obliged to do when the truth faces them. Brotherhood does not cease when the other person's opinions or dogmatics are different from one's own. As if there were not plenty of different dogmatics even in the New Testament, and as if our own dogmatics were not always outmoded in the next generation. When should we ever have the last word? Are not our own pupils, if not our contemporaries, teaching us where we have been blind? How lacking in greatness, nobility, humility, and teachableness those people usually are who are dominated by this slogan. How fearful they are lest they, to whom heaven and earth are promised, should have anything taken from them. How enclosed they still are, although Christ had to open the prison doors that barred their way. How they still hang on the words of the schoolmen and the church fathers, although the apostle expressly assures them that Paul and Apollos and Peter belong to them, too.

Protestants should therefore be allowed, with Roman Catholics and enthusiasts, to do whatever they are entitled to do in Jesus' name. How incessantly they create new parties and credal movements that speak of Christ in such a way that we can hear the shout behind it all: 'Great is Diana of the Ephesians!' (Acts 19.28). There is only one limit to what is allowed in Christian freedom; and that is not a theoretical but a practical one, although it ought then to be protected and clarified by a theory that is as good as possible, even if it is never complete. The limit of Christian freedom is 'and you are Christ's', which the enthusiasts did not hear then and did not want to hear. But neither have the valiant heresy-hunters, either of that time or of today, often heard it or wanted to hear it. Again and again they break through the boundary, staging the day of judgment on earth in a high-handed and often small-minded way, more suggestive of apologetic than of dogmatic charism. They would do better to leave that to the Lord who judges them, too, and who received tax-collectors and Zealots as his disciples. Even then, he had the experience of outraging the respectable citizens when he associated with prostitutes. He did not reject even those who could not believe that he would rise and had risen, as all the Easter narratives report. On the other hand, we have no business to organize the thousand years' Reich, and we ought to learn from politics, if not from church history, that that kind of thing always goes wrong, and that hell breaks loose afterwards, with the rise of Gog and Magog (Rev. 20.7f.). The thousand years' Reich is not our task; we have quite enough on hand with the affairs of today. 'And you are Christ's.' That, in our present time, can no longer be limited to our own little room, or to our family, or to the neighbourhood of our church spires. It means us in our world that is smaller and has become technical, threatened by atomic war, and pushing out into space travel. But at the same time it means us as individuals in our bodily nature. Only to him who belongs to Jesus of Nazareth is everything allowed and free.

Thus Paul contrasted his own theology of resurrection with that of the enthusiasts. His theology, too, is one of freedom; but it is that of people who are attached to Jesus, who are therefore distinguished by his cross, are called with him to suffer under the pious and the ungodly, under tyrants and institutions, are capable of brotherhood, and live on the strength of the first commandment. Its most important feature is that it is able to give freedom and to allow it to others. For it hands on what it has received, and thereby makes room for those who are caught in themselves and in their fears and sicknesses. Its business is to serve and help, and so it keeps alive the picture of Jesus. Thus far it remains directed towards earthly realities, instead of fleeing into heavenly realms. Jesus, too, came to those who needed him, and used his power so as to help them. This freedom is an anticipation of what things are to be like in the coming world and everlasting life. We talk of its being characterized by blessedness, and so we accommodate ourselves to the ideas and longings of other religions. That need not be wrong, but it is admissible only with one proviso: for us, blessedness is bound up with the sovereignty of Jesus. It is to be perfected in the future world, but it has already dawned on earth. If the freedom of the Christian man and the Christian church is centred on love, the resurrection of the dead is anticipated, because in it there appears the sovereignty of Jesus, which is perfected in the overcoming of death.

Everyone who is involved knows that the hardest struggle between so-called modern theology and church piety in Protestant Germany is over the message and hope of the resurrection of the dead. All the other points of difference come to a head here, and are judged from this angle. So it is possible to present a theology of resurrection against the allegedly unbelieving theology, and to conduct an intensive propaganda campaign on its behalf. The title of this chapter points to this controversy; and what has been said was intended to clarify it, even though it may not be adequate for ending it. Where there is smoke there is fire; and there is no doubt that many justified and unjustified assertions of critical theology, and especially the so-called existentialist interpretation, were bound to lead to the uneasiness that is gaining ground among us. I cannot here go into the historical, exegetical, and dogmatic problems of the message of the resurrection; to do so would need a separate book. It is obvious that I am, as a matter of course, on the side of thorough-going historical criticism, and, with certain reservations, on the side of an existentialist interpretation. But might it not seem that some of the controversy is not to the point, and that slogans are used that are at least questionable? Even the phrase 'theology of resurrection' as such is not clear. Just as in other religions, too, there is a theology of resurrection, so there was a collision, even in Corinth, between two different and incompatible Christian theologies of resurrection; and today we ought to be clear, from the outset, on which side of the former opponents we intend to come down.

That has not yet been decided, and the answer is by no means a foregone conclusion. The fact that people are hardly aware of the question suggests strongly that the firing is being done with blank cartridges. So I will set out once more the conclusions I have reached.

According to Paul, any theology of resurrection must not only start from christology but also remain with it. Anyone who gives prominence to soteriology and anthropology joins his Corinthian opponents, and now offers, at best, something like an antiquated philosophy. The resurrection of the dead is simply and solely a matter of Jesus' sovereignty over the earthly powers. Only as far as I share in Jesus' sovereignty may I speak, in a Christian sense, of the resurrection of the dead. If it is not testified to and verified in discipleship, its preaching and theology remain only the subject of argument; and as long as that is the case, there is no point in talking seriously about belief and unbelief. Of course, right doctrine is not unimportant; but there are two things that ought not to be forgotten for a moment. One is that the credibility of Christianity as a whole is at stake. Nothing is achieved here with right doctrine by itself. To put it in a heightened way, our hope in this case is something that we must see rather than just hear. The other is that we can 'see' only when, instead of nursing the expectation of our own survival and the end of the world, we serve Jesus as Lord.

Secondly, Paul has it that the rightness of any theology of resurrection must be shown by its speaking of the crucified Lord's sovereignty which makes us willing to bear the cross after him on earth. Anyone knowing merely the risen Lord who has left his cross behind is no longer speaking of Jesus of Nazareth, and so his theology of the resurrection can leave us cold. For no theology that does not lead us to Jesus deserves the term 'Christian', however interesting it may otherwise be. A theology of resurrection that does not become a theology of the cross is bound to lead, as the Corinthian example shows, to wrong-headed enthusiasm, and therefore to another form of the theology of glory against which the Reformation fought.

On earth, at any rate, there is no sharing in the glory of the risen Lord except in the discipleship of the cross. To put it forcibly : where Lazarus is raised, there is still floating in the air the smell of the corpse that has been rotting for four days. Anyone who tones this down does not know that resurrection, like birth, is a painful thing, and that the first impression given by a man coming out of the grave is one of terror. His theology of resurrection remains, at least on earth, a dream.

The third characteristic of resurrection as seen in a Christian light is that it takes place in the power of the first commandment. It therefore reveals the glorious liberty of the children of God, towards which, according to Rom. 8.21, the whole of world history is directed, because it is the real, permanent sign of the Son and his sovereignty. Any theology of resurrection which cannot speak of this liberty, which does not prepare the way for it, which prompts us to accept articles of faith but not to practise this liberty, misses the central point of the history of salvation and the world. We do, indeed, talk about our personal relationship to the exalted Lord, and by that we mean the possibility and reality of Christian prayer. But that merely shows how poverty-stricken and self-centred our faith has become. After all, non-Christians sometimes pray, and they, too, find lords in heaven and on earth, who comfort them. This, of course, is not said in order to decry prayer. What is vital is that the hope of resurrection should not end here, and that it should not be concentrated on serving private devoutness. The resurrection of the dead means a new world, and therefore creates a being who will no longer resign himself to the old conditions that now prevail on the earth. Thus there appears, even now, instead of the man shut up and ensnared in himself, the renewed man who stands in the ever-widening expanse of grace and the Spirit. Paul says tersely in II Cor. 3.17, 'Where the Spirit of the Lord is, there is freedom.' Ought that not to be the mark of every Christian life, every Christian community, and of Christianity as a whole? All doors are continually open to him who has and brings freedom, as we are told by the risen Jesus.

Our world is waiting for the revelation of the glorious liberty of the children of God. The fact that it turns away in such disappointment proves nothing against our Lord; but it does prove that we have still failed to give the world the right message and practice, however much we talk about the resurrection of the dead. For the most part, notwithstanding all our external and internal missionary work, which must not be broken off, we are a closed religious society. We certainly have to pray, and no prayer is more necessary than 'Come, creator Spirit!'. Then, however, we must take what is promised in answer to this prayer, namely the open expanse under heaven and on the earth, an expanse which no prison can deny us. The voice of free men cannot be suppressed; it still cries from its graves. Neither God nor men expect us to be perfect, but they demand that, under the cross of Jesus and in the strength of the first commandment, the travail should come about which leads to the birth of perfect freedom and to the heavenly Jerusalem, the mother of the free (Gal. 4.26). If we look at things in this way, we shall see that the real struggle has not yet begun in earnest. We are still contending more about philosophical presuppositions than about Paul's concern. Generally speaking, we let the theology of the cross and the theology of freedom play the part of Cinderella. But without them any theology of resurrection becomes, from a Christian point of view, an interesting (or boring) religious mental exercise of little substance or value.

4 Freedom according to the Church

The Epistle of James; the Pastoral Epistles; Ephesians

The post-Pauline New Testament writings are almost all involved in some kind of argument with the early Christian
enthusiasts, who were then within distance of disrupting the
churches and were compelling them everywhere to take stock
of their situation. What opposing parties said comes to us only
in brief and obscure allusions, so that for the most part we can
follow only the development that underlay the incipient early
catholicism. It is already an outward characteristic of that
development that the expression 'Christian freedom' had almost
completely disappeared. And indeed, if one is concerned for
order, the expression is generally inappropriate. We may note
two exceptions. In I Peter 2.16 the Christians are addressed as
free men who must not use their freedom as a pretext for evil,
because they remain servants of God. As often, I Peter echoes
a Pauline thought. The fact of our being at once children and
slaves of God is brought out dialectically, so as to exclude
irresponsible conduct. To be free one must also be obedient, as
only then can one remain harmoniously in the Father's house.
We shall not underestimate the force of such a verse; Paul's
main theological ideas continue to have their influence in the
mission field. On the other hand, if we realize the fact, the
limits of that influence are the more clearly defined. Freedom
is no longer the mighty river, carrying the whole life of the
Christian and the church, but a trickle that contributes, among
other things, to the community's instruction. Characteristically,
it emerges here when it is a question of establishing the duty
of the subject towards the authorities. Behind this is the Pauline

paradox that those who are really free serve, that the heirs of world domination submit to the existing earthly powers, that the eternal assumes the form of the temporal. Even those who are not familiar with the Pauline message will appreciate the attractive language in which he urges his readers to integrate themselves willingly in the political sphere.

Still more impressive is the phrase used in James 1.25 about 'the perfect law, the law of liberty', which is referred to again in 2.12, suggesting that we have here a phrase that had taken a firm hold in the tradition. The Epistle of James has many such phrases. Generally speaking, we see in the later New Testament the tendency that is also prevalent in present-day preaching and is often called, in a wider sense, the language of Canaan – the tendency to use pretty phrases instead of words expressing original and vigorous thought. Wherever they are found, they are adopted without regard to whether they still keep their former scope and depth; and instead of being a spiritual support, they become ornaments.

James 1.25 has also sometimes been thought to have a Pauline origin. That is not entirely out of the question, as 2.14ff. takes issue with some of Paul's misunderstood and perhaps extreme disciples. But we are not obliged to make the assumption, as the passage can quite easily be accounted for by the views and language of the Diaspora synagogue. It has assimilated the Stoic thesis, according to which the wise man participates in cosmic reason, and is to that extent inwardly a king and free. Judaism identifies with the divine law what the Stoics called cosmic reason, which asserts that one can live in thorough harmony with the order of things only if one knows and follows the law, because it is the voice of God. James, whose work may sometimes smack of slightly retouched Jewish traditions, takes this up and uses it to motivate his call to be a doer of the word. It is only in carrying out the message, which is now understood to be the new law, that one has a share in perfection and becomes truly free.

The exegesis of these passages is important for our subject, as it indicates a shift that will influence the whole history of the church. It is, indeed, not the great theologians who, on a long view, rule the churches, even though the latter may sometimes be called after them. They generally leave us a few memorable formulae and well-worn lines of thought. Then, after some time, the storms that led to mass movements subside. The church could save itself a great deal of agitation and anxiety by remembering what used to be said maliciously of the Austrian bureaucracy – that everything would settle itself in the end if one waited long enough. Regarded sociologically and historically, the great theologians are almost always fomentors of unrest, and their tactical and organizational detachment still forms part of the well-tried practices of ecumenical efforts. The enthusiasts' movements, however, slacken off in the course of a generation. People and institutions do not like to be kept continually on the alert, and they have constantly devised screens to protect themselves from too much heat. In fact, they have even managed to reduce Jesus' red-hot message, which promised to kindle a fire throughout the world, to room temperature. So they are now well able to deal with people who imagine God's reign to be somewhat explosive, dangerous, and breath-taking. In the same measure as the watchword of freedom recedes, there accumulate in the later period of early Christianity the admonitions to live a godly life in quietness and integrity. I am very far from wanting to ridicule this; on the contrary, it is advisable, even today, to break a lance for it on occasion, when unripe youth is too quick in sweeping it off the board.

On the other hand, we should remember that hardly any saying has so markedly shaped Christianity as has that about godliness in quietness and integrity; it has been combined intolerably with the political maxim that calmness is the citizen's first duty. It has become so generally axiomatic that Christians could not be revolutionaries, that no one now takes offence if they become reactionary; in fact, it is regarded as normal and in line with God's will. When, as generally happens, the old Adam swings back from extremes to the centre after certain extravagances, we ought not to regard it as meritorious in all circumstances for the new Adam to behave in the same way. Very often it is only the heart's indolence which, according to the story of the Emmaus road, can spread itself even in the shade of the resurrection events. But that is the kind of thing that happens when one puts the whole of the Bible on the same plane and condemns historical criticism as godless. It does not mean at all that we should accept everything as having equal weight; we leave whole sections of the Bible more or less unregarded, even if we still read them. We are constantly choosing and separating the essential from the peripheral according to our own taste, although we severely condemn other people for making subjective judgments. Devout people are no less inclined to contradiction than are the children of the world, although they are apt to be less critical of themselves, and for the most part less inclined to laugh at themselves. Any cases of toning down that occur in early Christian times need cause us no offence; they may help us immeasurably in our own lives if we regard the human as well as the divine in Scripture and history.

The distinguished exegete Martin Dibelius once said of the Pastoral Epistles, to Timothy and Titus, that they mark the beginning of the bourgeois outlook in the church. I do not think that is a very happy way of putting it, though it does draw attention most aptly to the obvious symptom of a shifting of emphasis. We have to picture to ourselves the danger in which Christianity stood at the time. Imperial Rome had not yet stepped in, although its menace was everywhere and might already be felt in the chicanery practised by some of the lower courts. The church was no longer exposed to acts of repression by the Jews; the danger came rather from the competition of pagan religiosity. But the assaults of the enthusiast led almost to the disintegration of the church from within, and so doors had to be bolted against them everywhere. Whereas the Epistles of John call for solidarity in brotherly love when confronted with them, II Peter defends traditional eschatology against them. He does so in such a way that early Christian prophecy is greatly restricted, and the exposition of Scripture is reserved for the ecclesiastical office, which is traced back to the apostolic succession. Elsewhere, as in I Peter and probably in James, the Christian's ethical duty is specially emphasized.

It was in that setting that the Pastoral Epistles drew up systematic rules for the churches of Paul's former mission field. The church's stability, organization, and criteria were becoming an urgent problem. That was especially so in Paul's sphere of work, as his preaching always had a magnetic attraction for restless spirits. His churches do not seem to have remained for long in the form that he gave them. Where they were not completely wrecked by the enthusiasts, they had to have fixed regulations prescribed for them on Jewish-Christian lines. We can already see in Colossians and II Thessalonians what a stormy course was taken by theological arguments. Lastly, Ephesians is the classical document of church doctrine shaped from the Pauline inheritance. At the same time, we cannot regard as Pauline the development by which the church, in its ecumenical breadth and with its ecumenical features, became the central theme of theology. A hymn to it, arranged on a pattern that was originally christological, introduces the letter in a way befitting the passage in 5.23ff., where the relation of Christ to the church is understood as the great mystery of the last days and as a prototype of Christian marriage. Here the gospel is domesticated. In future, the world may be its sphere. But it is so only as the frame into which the picture of the church fits, and on that picture rests all the splendour to which even the end of history can contribute nothing essential. Christology is integrated with the doctrine of the church. The head is present only with and through the body. Christ is the mark towards which Christianity is growing, and no longer in the strict sense its judge.

The church as the real content of the gospel, its glory the boundless manifestation of the heavenly Lord, sharing in it being identical with sharing in Christ and his dominion, his qualities being communicable to it – we know that message. It has lasted for two thousand years, has fascinated Protestantism, too, and is today the main driving force of the ecumenical movement. If only the theology of the cross were brought in to counterbalance it! But the church triumphant, even if it starts from the cross and guards it as its most precious mystery, has still always stood in a tense relationship to the crucified Lord himself. As long as the tension remained alive in it under violent friction, one could in some degree come to terms with the situation. The greatest danger always arose when the church pushed itself into the foreground so that Christ's image above it faded into an image of the founder, of the cultic hero, or became an ecclesiastical icon to be put side by side with other icons that were set up from time to time. It was against that danger that the Reformation in fact rose up, not against the secularization of the church, although the two things necessarily went together. Where the world is dominated by the church, and even Christ is integrated in its metaphysical system, the church becomes conversely a religiously transfigured world. Its real Babylonian captivity, however, consists in its making itself the focal point of salvation and the theme of the gospel. The church's introversion puts it into the sharpest contrast with the crucified Lord who did not seek his own glory and gave himself to the ungodly.

It is right and proper that we should here and now warn German Protestantism most urgently of this danger, for here it has everything, namely itself, to lose. An ecumenical movement that revolves round the church's teaching and aspires to achieve unification on that basis, ends in Rome. That is not to say anything against the ecumenical movement as such, which I think we are required, not only to support, but to strive for with all our might. Nor is it to say anything against that Roman Catholicism in whose critical youth I sometimes think I have more friends and brethren than in my own camp. Why, indeed, should not the last handshake as a sign of reconciliation be exchanged in Rome just as well as anywhere else, although for the present any such expectation seems to be quite utopian? One has to make the sign of the cross for protection from oneself and from those who encourage our old Adam. But demons lie in wait everywhere, and unfor-

tunately they are not so easily outflanked by Christians as the
gospel is. With Rome, here is the symbol of the church which
chooses to make itself absolute, and which in its tradition, its
official capacity, and its legal claims, avoids the judgment of
the crucified Lord. We cannot accept that mother and school-
mistress of the faithful, who robs Christ of his titles and remains
the opponent of the reforming *particula exclusiva*. It is right
and proper for us to give warning of the approaching danger
to which we may long since have fallen victims. For we, for
our part, are also heirs of a continuing history, even if we disregard the Reformation and merely look at what has begun
with us since the last century.

It began with Vilmar and Löhe and the other Neo-Lutherans
who rediscovered the church for themselves and their time,
with the Erlangen theologians who produced the catchword
'salvation history', with the worthy liberals such as Deissmann,
Bousset, and Fridrichsen, who suddenly took to cultic piety. It
went on with Erik Petersen and Otto Dibelius; the latter proclaimed the century of the church and thereby drew on himself derision that was both justified and, in view of the development, unjustified. Then, to mention only a few names, Schlier
and Bonhoeffer and I took up, each in his own way, the legacy
that came from such diverse sources. In the extreme north
there was approval because the most important theological
development of our time was thought to have set in. It is not as
if we were speaking as blind people speak of colour. When the
ecumenical movement was still in its infancy, our hearts
warmed to the theme of the church, and unfortunately our
heads did not keep cool. We know what course the matter took
with Petersen and Schlier. We others did not go their way –
whether through inconsistency or because of bitter experiences. For a broad way leads, not only to hell, but also from
anthropology to ecclesiology! – it keeps on surprising me
afresh. We were swimming so happily with the current, and
we could have entirely avoided our present ill-repute by continuing to do so. Crypto-Catholicism is respected everywhere
today, especially when it keeps a few emblems of the Reforma-

tion. There is little to be urged on its behalf except what we already felt or told ourselves in our salad days, when other people were still quite satisfied with themselves as liberal or orthodox Protestants. We are familiar with their latest fashions, and we are not thinking of buying from them what, in view of our unforeseen course, now looks like a drug on the market, taken out of old stock. If that gives us a bad reputation, we will at least add to it the contempt that burnt children may show for those who see them heedlessly take hold of live coals.

We have come back to the *particula exclusiva*, some more, some less, but in that direction. We have done so because, after the exciting discovery of the church, we made the even more exciting discovery of the crucified Lord. We may let other people decide whether such an antithesis is right or wrong. For us it is the outcome of our life and work, and even if it is biassed and subjective, it is now irreversible. One must finally land somewhere, and one must not worry if others think they can see better landing-places. We still attach great weight to church doctrine, as we do to the ecumenical movement, and even to Catholicism. We are willing to devote time and energy to them; but they no longer fascinate us, because no theology of glory is able to fascinate us any longer. We do not deny that there always (though not everywhere) has been and will be a holy Christian church. But that has to be demythologized always and everywhere, and so related to reality and function. Dogmatically, the demythologizing of the church is the crucial point for demythologizing the canon. Without the church we should become wandering nomads. Without it, not even the partisans can live. But it is no other than the brotherhood of those who invoke Christ as Lord, follow him, and serve him throughout the world. Their sole glory is that they are allowed to serve him.

From this we may even interpret and accept the mystical passage about the bride in Eph. 5. But we must admit that we do not feel happy at this mystical presentation, which brings along Christ and the church teamed up together in heaven and makes them jointly the prototype of Christian marriage. There is only one Being who is enthroned in heaven, and with that reflection of the earthly community in the heavenly sphere there begins the earthly catastrophe of false authority and ecclesiastical self-worship. It leads to the inquisitions and public claims to jurisdiction by a Christianity that has been called only to serve. We have reason to maintain our protest against this, at least among Protestants, when necessary, just as the iconoclasts have reason to destroy the fictitious painted halo. Anyone whose life has been influenced by the church struggle ought always to remember, in his ecclesiology, the scene described in Ezra 3.10ff.: while the people were rejoicing at the laying of the foundation of the temple, 'many of the priests and Levites and heads of fathers' houses, old men who had seen the first house, wept. . . .', and so the rejoicing and the loud weeping were inextricably mixed. No one should be debarred from praising the church, and such praise ought by all means to be encouraged in the right place and within suitable limits. The longing for the place where the saints forgather and the beautiful divine services are celebrated may well be inextinguishable within us; and we must not cultivate spirituality by despising organizations and their rules and needs. But no ecclesiology is Protestant that does not involve loud and unmistakable weeping over the earthly Zion. Here there is no need for us to be moved by the ideals of those who have seen the glory of the old temple; it would be better for us to listen to Rev. 21.22, which tells us why the heavenly city will have no temple: 'Its temple is the Lord God the Almighty and the Lamb.' The church is always and everywhere liable to be brought to an end at some future time. There will remain at the last only the Lord and his people, and the people will no longer worship in Jerusalem or on Mount Gerizim, but in spirit and in truth. Because that is how things are, we say that the church must constantly be reforming itself, and even more, must incessantly outstrip itself.

In the ecumenical age one does not fail to notice unrest and new departures everywhere. The so-called modern theology

ought to be integrated here, instead of being judged by the
old. For many young people the sole attraction of the church
is its unrest – certainly not fully fermented, but alive – and
its resolute departure into God's unknown future. We ourselves know better than those who lament our action what
unavoidable dangers lie in our way. It does not tell in their
favour, but rather against them, that they have still not realized
that the journeyings of God's people take place in the desert,
are a constant experiment, and are bound to end in failure
unless they are protected by grace. By the same token, we
regret that the Reformation churches no longer lead the forward march, but embark on experiments only under pressure,
hesitantly, timidly, and unprepared to give up their own lives.
Those who talk the most loudly about God's Spirit are the least
likely to be urged on by him. Where people used to be just
conservative, they have now very largely become reactionary.
Symptoms of this can be seen everywhere. Ecclesiastical statements are produced on the assembly line; and for the most
part even their style shows them to be out of date. We ought
to leave pathos to those who do not blow the wrong trumpet.
The Barmen Declaration – 'We confess', 'we repudiate' –
gives no evidence of the right spirit. Confessions can really be
written only through blood and tears. Ecclesiastical pronounce-
ments would be adequate to their present situation if they
kept away from holy oil, were essentially informative, and at
all costs avoided platitudes with which no one could disagree.
As is the case with the average sermon, one always knows in
advance what is coming next.

But really, that no longer needs to be said. The world does
not listen now, even if we sing psalms every day of the week.
No one but its guardians of the established order is still happy
about our prevailing patriarchalism and all the hieratical
mumbo-jumbo. The suddenly increasing pious respect for the
chief ecclesiastical offices leads to a grotesque result if it means
that the chief administrative officials also receive excessive
deference. From the Protestant point of view there is only
one such office – that of the gospel message, to which every

Christian is called. It is all put over the same denominator: the numinous is demonstrated in the sphere of the secular. Instead of that, Jesus showed the numinous by entering into the secular. The worst of it is that people do not notice any such contrast, and try actually to serve God in a lack of understanding, by cultivating sacred ceremonies. That began in I Tim. 3.15, where the church was proclaimed to be the pillar and bulwark of the truth. No objection need be raised to that as long as the church is in fact so, as indeed it often enough and long enough has been. But people have become used to seeing the church exclusively in that light, although it has repeatedly become the bulwark of religious rituals, changing from an emergency building to a world-wide super-structure, from servant to mistress.

How did the situation come about that we regard as the real cause of offence – namely, that the church was identified with the reign of God and regarded as the earthly representa-tive of the power of Christ? The answer, briefly stated, is: because of urgency and necessity. Urgency and necessity are always the really productive situations, although they are certain to provoke dangers too. That is true of the Epistle to the Ephesians. Its lofty concept of the ecumenicity of Jewish and Gentile Christians arose from the difficulty that the expanding mission to the Gentiles pushed the Jewish Christians further and further into the background, so that they finally became a small sect apart and an easy prey for Islam. The truly inspired writer of the letter had a misfortune of that kind before his eyes, and sought with his enthusiastic programme to prevent it. The Pastoral Epistles are concerned with the other urgent matter, the problem of the enthusiasts. They tackled it in an appropriately unenthusiastic and even anti-enthusiastic way by tightening the church organization and taking the field against the extremists.

A brief outline may suffice, although here, as elsewhere, we shall have to ignore many problems that could be dealt with adequately only in large books. Essentially, the subject matter will be found in three intersecting circles, the most important question probably being that of church administration. It was solved by introducing the episcopate everywhere, with a graduated ecclesiastical hierarchy ranging from deacons to widows, who were given their own defined duties. The ecclesiastical office was guarded in two ways: in fact, at any rate, it was made a matter of apostolic succession by virtue of ordination; this was mediated by the apostolic pupils Timothy and Titus. Besides this, the charismata were partly institutionalized, and in any case brought into line with the apostolic office, so that they lost their earlier independence. Whatever did not fit into that framework was therefore eliminated. That means, in the second place, that preaching, which had previously been the prerogative of anyone who was inspired, was brought under control. That control rested again with the bishop, even if he alone exercised authority over doctrine and exposition. That left room only for what was formally allowed under such control. The object that was aimed at, and no doubt the result that was widely attained, was 'sound doctrine' that was at once normative and regulative. In the third place, the churches saw themselves, above all, as a model of 'God's family', with corresponding importance attached to the building up of the Christian family. It was, so to speak, the germ-cell for God's family taken as a whole. Thus a patriarchal system took root.

It was therefore not so much a question, as Dibelius thought, of turning the church into a bourgeois society, although it may seem so to us. It was really a matter of stabilizing the conditions in a chaotic environment. We cannot deny the greatest respect to this undertaking, for the procedure that was followed was appropriate, and what was appropriate in the church's organization might well coincide with what was pleasing to God. We may even say, perhaps with some slight exaggeration, that in this way the Christian church adapted itself to the reconstructive programme in which the empire in general was engaged. In its own sphere it was impressively successful. It is no trifling matter when, in a disintegrating world, the Christian community achieves and maintains order, and through its mere presence calls to mind the good will of the Creator. Of course, the reverse side of the medal must not be overlooked. As in human affairs generally, so in the church, too, what was established acquired an importance of its own, the halo of legitimacy, wrung from the urgency of the situation and to that extent necessary. Castles of defence into which one flees from danger become castles of defiance from which one cannot break away when the time comes to change from the defensive to the offensive. The little band had seen its salvation in discipline; but discipline soon began to use the rod. Once a person is compelled to get used to living in a cramped space, narrow-mindedness follows almost inevitably. The Pastoral Epistles and their historical after-effects provide excellent material for a study of all this.

The church's necessity demanded order. But in spite of all protestations to the contrary, order is not a specifically Christian concept, and not even an inalienable Christian value, as peace between God and man is. This is shown in the Pastoral Epistles by the fact that the order that they aspire to and in fact establish has to be backed by sanctions. The apostolic succession of the episcopal office is, to put it quite plainly – of course, I can speak only in the name of historical criticism – one of the many Christian fictions. There is only one apostolic succession that can be authenticated beyond all doubt, and that is discipleship of Jesus. It is quite true that the church of the Pastorals, like the letters themselves, can appeal to Paul, or at least to one side of the apostle that they could understand. But Paul by no means represents the apostolate in general. In the Pastoral Epistles his image is heavily daubed by church piety, his theology is levelled out, and his main concerns are misunderstood. He was also an organizer, but that was a secondary matter to him, and a rather hasty one, and here he always had to be vigorously helped along by what had been inherited from Jewish Christianity. When he tried to safeguard and enforce discipline, the urgency exhibited in his letters shows very clearly that he was unsuccessful all his life. That was partly his own fault, because he did not yet link the charismata with an ecclesiastical office, but with the Spirit's good judgment and with love, and these proved, even among Christians, to be uncertain aids. He certainly used Hellenistic material of the popular philosophical kind, besides Jewish tradition, as models for Christian ethics in everyday life. But they were not derived from any comprehensive regulative principle, and therefore did not appear simple to the new Christian law. Nor did he reduce the gospel to the sound doctrine that had to take on the features of a normal theology. In the wake of traditional thought people mainly stress the points of agreement between him and his later disciples. But what is at least as important is what the latter had forgotten or simply no longer had the power to keep.

Only then do we realize how the basic change that has meantime taken place in theology and practice is conclusively expressed: where urgency and necessity call like that for order, it does not by any means follow that Christian freedom is simply got rid of. But that freedom is taken under control, and in a way under direction. The Spirit defines dialectically what the church is, only so far as the church for its part at the same time defines the Spirit. Even that must not be put out of court as long as Spirit and church cannot be severed from one another. But if the Spirit is essentially defined by the church as a component part of order, not only is enthusiasm banished, but the church, as the guardian and custodian of the Spirit, is no longer subject to a higher authority by which it is itself judged. The Spirit, in fact, becomes the force of the tradition ruling in the church; and the fiction is then indispensable that that tradition is homogeneous. But our rapid survey from Jesus to Jewish Christianity and the Hellenistic church and Paul has already demonstrated how heterogeneous the church's tradition actually was. It is not to be forgotten how many struggles, antagonisms, and splinterings shaped it, and how explosive was the mixture that finally resulted from what was accepted here, there, or generally. But a Christianity that lives on fictions has to introduce, if not the law, at least legality. That becomes all the worse if it does so in the name of the Spirit; it makes the freedom of the Christian man grievous. There is freedom only in so far as one submits to the prevailing regulations of the church – that is, in the private sphere.

Of course, that sphere will be sanctioned and illumined in its religious aspect, and will be characterized by godliness and integrity. To make Christian freedom a private affair is not to abolish it; but it means that fundamentally freedom is only a claim and an honour of the church as such. It has become domesticated, or, if one may coin the word, churchified. From now on, the church fights for its freedom both inwardly and outwardly, but it can no longer call itself seriously and exclusively, as Adolf Schlatter did, the company of free people. That is the price that Christian people have paid, and still pay, for the maintenance of order. Even in Protestantism, the freedom of the Christian man and of the church as a whole has become a catchword. The favourite occasions of its use are church feasts, whereas in everyday life it is always regarded with considerable reserve through a not unreasonable fear of arbitrary power. Now we are so used to order that Christian freedom, unless it is interpreted on that basis, almost borders on insurrection. Walls have become ever closer, and hearts ever narrower. Our thinking, in so far as we have not left it entirely to people called on to do it for us, has grown more and more provincial, and Christianity has become a supporting pillar (now rather fragile) of the bourgeois society. To take suitable action in an emergency is one thing. To turn what is necessary on a single occasion into something unchangeable is another. Have we not shut ourselves up intolerably within what is old, conventional, and time-honoured, and turned ourselves into a religious ghetto in relation to other people? Has not the price of the church order that we have gained been too high after all, once the days of the enthusiasts and the persecution were over? Do we not need a root and branch reformation for the sake of what is appropriate, necessary and urgent today? Today the church alone, as a company of free people, has the promise that it shall glorify Jesus' name before the world and carry out its appointed service in the world. As a kind of religious field for exercising power and instituting order it has long since been overtaken in secular matters. It can therefore only adopt an introverted attitude in collecting and preserving the things peculiar to it – things that are melting away faster and faster. And whatever freedom the church represents and claims ecumenically remains ideological in so far as it is not based on and manifested in the freedom of the Christian man. We have to learn again that in the everyday life of secularism every single Christian represents the church. For that, however, one must offer something more than order – namely, the disciple's freedom that is the fruit of the Spirit.

5 The Long Road

The Epistle to the Hebrews: Luke-Acts

The Epistle to the Hebrews describes the church as God's people on the march in the last days. Through earthly affliction it is in danger of collapse and apostasy from the faith. For here faith means faithfulness. The whole letter is an admonition not to yield to temptation. According to 10.35ff. we must not throw away confidence and patience. In the struggle to which we have been committed we must, according to 12.1ff., resist even to martyrdom; 12.12f. bids us lift our drooping hands and strengthen our weak knees, as the day of final deliverance is not far off. For God has promised his people rest, the Sabbath that he himself celebrated after the creation. According to 12.22ff. the festal gathering is already taking place on the heavenly Mount Zion, with innumerable angels and 'just men made perfect' round the divine judge, and Jesus as the mediator of the new covenant. If people of the desert once approached Sinai to hear the terrifying revelation of the conclusion of the first covenant, they are now standing within sight of the heavenly Jerusalem, where eternal salvation awaits us. That makes the earthly 'today', which is stressed in 2.7ff., all the more significant; it indicates both the extreme danger and the glorious promise that is soon to be fulfilled. Such a dividing line can be crossed only by one who continually listens to God's living word.

The Epistle was written by an unknown teacher. For the most part, we cannot identify the writers of the New Testament books, the great exception being Paul, who allows us to penetrate so deeply into his history. Of the writers of the Gospels, Acts, and Revelation we know nothing but the names.

It is quite out of the question that they could have been disciples of the early Jesus; for they already had to collect the traditions about their Lord. They read the Old Testament in the Greek translation, and the conditions reflect the destruction of Jerusalem. Lastly, the non-Pauline letters, as probably those to the Colossians and Ephesians and II Thessalonians, are pseudonymous. That does not mean that we have to speak of forgery. It was a common practice to use an apostle's name to indicate that one was an heir to authentic tradition as opposed to false doctrine. Of course, that soon became useless; opponents quickly realized the value of such a signboard and introduced the most dubious notions, suitably camouflaged, into the church. So from the second century onwards there was an incessant and increasing output of apocryphal and pseudonymous sayings of Jesus, gospels, epistles, and revelations. We can see from this that the border-line between orthodoxy and heresy remained fluid for a long time, and that a painstaking process of elimination was needed for compiling the recognized canon. We can also see from this that the New Testament itself does not favour the theory of apostolic succession.

The only man about whom we know a good deal for certain is Paul; and according to his letters his apostleship, and even his Christianity, was already being contested in his own lifetime and in his own churches. Anyone who would back up the true gospel by names, the bearers of ecclesiastical offices, and canonical authorities, is on the wrong track. God's affairs can never be justified, supported, or unequivocally proved through human beings, traditions, alleged or actual historical facts, or even through Christianity as such. The most that we can obtain by such means is a helpful community that is essential to us in our search for truth. We need witnesses who can point out to us the one thing necessary. But on the other hand, witnesses will always say different things and contradict each other, showing that Christianity has constantly had different and even contrasting aspects. In the last resort, therefore, each of us is left to answer for his own faith or superstition; we cannot acquire any standing in God's sight through our company or our party or our creed. Nor can we let other people represent us in this matter, for majorities are dangerous rather than serviceable to truth. The testimony of the Holy Spirit in our conscience is indispensable, and – provided we pay proper regard to other courts of appeal, and especially if we are in constant and careful touch with Scripture – it must have the last word. Nowhere in our life are we spared the glorious freedom, but also the temptation, of God's children; we have to enter into both, even when we consult the canon, which in the absence of the Spirit is not, and does not remain, God's word. In the same way, no letter from parents, children, or friends will convince anyone of love unless he, too, loves, although but for those letters his love may become cold and dry.

The writer of the Epistle to the Hebrews is an early Christian teacher. That status, as well as that of prophet, is evidence that the gospel belongs to a definite point in history; but the teacher holds more closely to current tradition. So the Epistle's message is supplied by two main sources, namely, the acknowledgment of Christ (probably proclaimed at baptism), and the sacred writings of the Old Testament. We have already spoken of the origin of the christological confessions among the enthusiasts, and we have seen that their characteristic belief was that the conqueror of death and the devil brings his disciples through his own strength into his victory. The writer to the Hebrews modifies this idea significantly, no doubt in accordance with the traditions of his time. For him Jesus remains God's eternal Son, who co-operated even in the world's creation and preserves it by his word. After his abasement, the cross and resurrection have brought him back to heaven, where he now rules till the day of judgment. But in this connection the earthly Lord's suffering is given unusual importance, as is clearly expressed in 2.10: 'For it was fitting that he, for whom and by whom all things exist, in bringing many sons to glory, should make the pioneer of their salvation perfect through suffering.' The Creator treats his Son just as he treats his people. He reveals in the cross his method of teaching all his children, and even Jesus is not exempted from it. Thus far it is simply the token of God over history: 'Amid sorrows the Master imprints his all-prevailing image on hearts and minds.' 5.8f. puts it still more precisely: 'Although he was a Son, he learned obedience through what he suffered; and being made perfect he became the source of eternal salvation to all who obey him.' Here, in a play on words that cannot be exactly reproduced, the writer takes up the motto succinctly expressed by the Greek tragedian Aeschylus in the words: 'Learn by suffering'. Hebrews contains maxims of that kind mediated through Jewish wisdom; and from here also comes the reference to divine teaching, which is not a central theme of the New Testament, but was later to become a *leitmotif*.

The climate of the early Christian message had obviously changed. As long as people were reckoning every day on the immediate coming of God's reign, or, like the Corinthians, were already celebrating it, they did not reflect about the fate of mankind and earthly distress in general. The comforting words were enough: 'Behold, I make all things new'. Temporal affliction could not well be overlooked; Adam's fall and the buffetings of fate on the long road that God's people had travelled were not forgotten. But those events formed the background of the night that was coming to an end, the night that was suddenly to be interrupted by the cry: 'Look up and raise your heads, because your redemption is drawing near' (Luke 21.28). But it gradually had to be admitted that the day of judgment was a long time in coming; and then the old questioning about the meaning of life was renewed, even among Christians. People thankfully adopted Old Testament Jewish wisdom, which told of God's work in educating the earth and mankind. It is indeed true that suffering may make people stubborn and rebellious, just as it may lead to reflection and profitable experience. But anyone who has been able to reconcile himself at all to his lot will agree that nothing is more favourable to growth and maturity than suffering steadfastly borne. Faith will see God there as the educator.

We can go a step further. There is nothing new, either, in the theme of Jesus' obedience, in which Rom. 5.12ff. and Phil. 2.6ff. saw the glory of the earthly Christ. But again the writer to the Hebrews follows a different track; he does not regard Jesus' obedience as the antithesis of the disobedience of Adam's world and as the mark of Jesus' uniqueness. It is the sign of that humility which unites the Son with us, and of a universally valid law : 'Learn by suffering'. According to Paul, too, the Son creates sons, the Obedient One creates obedient people; and so the disciples are urged to become like their Lord in suffering. But the apostle speaks of the manifestation of the new obedience, which bears the stamp of the new world. Since Christ there has once more been an earth that listens to its Creator. In Hebrews the line of argument changes significantly : Jesus, too, had to submit to the law that rules us. In his passion he shared in our fate and became like us, so that we could follow confidently in his steps. In other words, he became our model. To be sure, he towers above all other models, and so, in 12.2, he is called 'the pioneer and perfecter of our faith'. That expression is not entirely new; indirectly it underlies the stories of Jesus' temptation, of Gethsemane, part of the passion narrative, and in particular the song of God's servant, in I Peter 2.21ff. For all that, the New Testament in general does not go to Jesus for the essence of faith. He is not a model for faith, but the Lord of the believers.

It is here that one may rightly criticize a theology that would find the entire gospel in co-humanity. Certainly, Christian faith paradoxically unites an 'I may' with an 'I ought to'. But that is possible even in Judaism and Hellenism, and still more so in the philosophy of, shall we say, Kant and Fichte, which was influenced by Christianity. We therefore have to set out clearly, from a theological point of view, whether and how far what is Christian can be identical with what is ideally human. It is only if we say 'Yes' that we can and may, in a supposedly post-Christian epoch, resolve it in a humanistic movement.

The answer must be 'No'. Otherwise we should have to say that Jesus' cross amounted to nothing more than part of the common experience of human brutality and earthly suffering. We should have to see in him simply an example of God's pedagogy that is preached in Jewish wisdom and taken up again, amply and uncritically, in the message of the ancient church. Of course, in thinking of the crucified Lord we may reflect on real humanity. But it would be inadmissible arrogance to be so exclusive as to justify a reflexion of that kind merely by regarding the cross by itself and commandeering humanism on behalf of Christianity. It may also be legitimate to describe Jesus as the pioneer and perfecter of our faith, for Christian faith is actually tied wholly to Jesus. If such language is used with the intention of honouring Jesus as the creator of faith, there is no objection to it. But theology is not just a matter of intentions. It has no honour or urgency if it defends formulations on the basis of the intentions that they proclaim; on the contrary, it has to appraise the statements critically, having regard to their purposes, their appropriateness, and their dangers.

So the freedom that is preached on the basis of Jewish, Greek, or philosophical thought is to be distinguished from that preached by the gospel. The norm for it cannot be the effect achieved, or supposed to be achieved, on man, however important it is. An 'I may' and 'I ought to' may win over, or lay claim to, different people differently; but that does not mean that it is valid as a norm. Again, we ought on no account to despise a Christianity that becomes a religious variety of humanism. What more could Christians want than that humanism should at last become a world-wide decisive reality instead of an often misused slogan? Nevertheless the evangelical norm for all preaching is still the christological question: Do we know Jesus? To make him the model, and even the archetype, of our own nature, will not satisfy our faith. He certainly opens out to us a view of our own existence, but he does more than that. The New Testament certainly calls him the firstborn among many brethren, but he is always more than that. He teaches us to know that Creator who wants the new world and brings it about by judging the old world. He remains our Lord, who makes the first commandment, in its promise as well as in its prohibition, the basis and frontier of our life.

Nietzsche, with the fine flair of the combative hater, rightly realized that even idealistic humanism must break up on the cross. It is no accident that, according to I Cor. 1.23, the Greeks reject the cross as foolishness, and that in the Hellenistic world Christianity was regarded as something to be hated by the whole human race. Not without reason has genuine humanism in all epochs turned away in disgust from Jesus' cross. It rightly saw that the preaching that glorified the cross denied the dignity of man, and it held the proclamation that a crucified person was Lord and God to be perverse and blasphemous. Jesus teaches us by divine authority to protect and respect what is human, but he does not base one's own respectability on that; otherwise we should have to think of him only as a teacher, and make his story a human tragedy. There is a humanism that is the fruit of life and of Jesus' teaching and death; what it cannot be is a vehicle of christology. For all humanism, the scandal of the cross as the saving event is insuperable. Christian preaching of the cross is in a sense thoroughly inhuman, for it strips a man of his assumed dignity and unmasks him, not merely as a beggar, but as a criminal before God. Those who feel it to be an offence understand it better and more seriously than those who give it an exclusively humanistic direction and boundary. Paul, John, the reformers, and indeed Jesus himself maintained that our righteousness and wisdom, as well as our piety, are ended when God comes on the scene. When that happens, we may know that we are bound up in co-humanity with all creatures. But there is no such thing as Christian humanism, any more than there is a Christian State or the Christian West. Anyone who asserts the contrary suffers from illusions, and idealizes the past from which the present has come. When Christians stand up for humanism, culture, and better politics, let them do so from the dividing line marked by the cross, and remember that there is no service without offence.

What does this mean for our analysis of the Epistle to the Hebrews? We have seen that it takes up the early Christian creed; it does so in order to comfort the church that was being tempted, and to call on it to stand fast; and so the creed became an occasion for it to emphasize Jesus' example. We now have to realize the danger of that emphasis. When we speak of the cross as included in the divine pedagogy, we do not take away its offence. Both are removed into the realm of the suffering that we undergo, and therefore into the realm of pious humanity. It is not by chance that Jewish wisdom gives the point of view and the horizon for this presentation, which sees the appointed way to perfection as through suffering. The rule is, in fact, valid here (though with Paul it is otherwise): through cross to crown. That is very effective pastorally, and it became a permanent theme of all subsequent preaching. But if Jesus, too, is brought under this rule, the anthropological result takes the edge off the christological offence: his cross simply has no place in any pedagogy, where it is a matter of interpreting what is apparently meaningless, of the sequence of phases of development, of the transcendence of what is most human, and lastly of the transfiguration of what is humane by fitting it into a celestial plan of salvation. In Jesus' cross an end is made of all earthly running and striving, from which there can follow only the new creation out of nothing, or else despair. Its effect is to break up man before his Lord.

The early Christian creed not only gave the Epistle the chance of emphasizing Jesus' suffering and therefore the development that produced the story of the passion as the first stage in the formation of the gospel. Rom. 8.34 shows that the theme of the high priest who represents us before God had already been put forward. The letter develops this piece of early Christian liturgy very amply in long chapters. Here again, the pastoral interest is dominant: the church's salvation is guaranteed by him who is continually interceding for us with the Father. That is most intimately associated with Jesus' passion; the heavenly high priest is constantly reminding God of the sacrifice made at Golgotha. It is held present for ever, so to speak, as it is delineated on earth in the Lord's Supper, of which we are reminded in the eucharistic language of 13.10ff. Nowhere in the New Testament is the view of Jesus' supreme sacrifice as an atonement for our sins more clearly reflected.

As this view provides the second important point of controversy between ecclesiastical piety and modern theology, we have to look at the matter more closely. We can begin by making two assertions that may help to relax any tension that the discussion might produce. Here, too, it is apparent that Paul's line of thought differs from that of Hebrews. For the apostle, Jesus' death is the completion of that obedience which inaugurates the new obedience in the world of Adam, and with it establishes the new creation. Freedom from the unconquerable power of sin is stressed here; and for that purpose we are also reminded on occasion, as in Rom. 3.24f., of the Jewish-Christian message of Jesus' sacrificial death as the liberation from the burden of sin. To Jewish Christianity, in whose succession the Epistle to the Hebrews stands, the forgiveness of former guilt was of supreme importance. So 'sins' were spoken of, in the plural. Paul, on the other hand, is concerned to show that the power of sin (in the singular) no longer prevents us from living a new life in the service of Christ; the two are not incompatible. In one case one looks more backwards to the past; in the other case, more forwards to the future – the stress is different. That ought to make us reflect that in early Christianity things were not yet laid down, as people sometimes want them today, according to one single idea and method of preaching.

The second difference is still more important. The main interest of the Epistle to the Hebrews is in what the heavenly high priest does for his own people in the present time. He intercedes for them with the Father by reminding him of Golgotha. Here we can see clearly that the letter deliberately picks out the fact of representation from the theme of the sacrificial death. Jesus is the mediator between God and man. As he reveals the Father's will to us, so he commends us to the Father. Here, too, the idea of offence, which is such a basic element in Paul's preaching of the cross, is absent. On the contrary, the Epistle explains Jesus' sacrificial death by making it the end, and the final logical sequel to Old Testament sacrifices. There is a whole series of actions preceding and pointing to Jesus' death; and however greatly it overtops them, it nevertheless finishes their sequence. It is unique in the sense of its surpassing greatness, but not at all in regard to the feeling of offence that blatantly confronts our forebodings and wishes. Paul does not consider that men with their cultic activities have always been pointing ahead to Golgotha. On the contrary, at Golgotha everything that had previously been regarded as piety went down in ruin. The God who breaks the will even of devout people makes all man's handiwork and all earthly ritual vain and foolish. He does not crown our efforts with his grace, but actually judges our piety by his grace. The apostle contrasts the enormity of the plan of salvation with its pedagogy. What a God, to whom men can offer nothing, because he fashions his work out of chaos with unserviceable material (II Cor. 3.5)! What a picture of man, who is not only always a beggar, but a criminal against his Lord as well! Anyone who wants to talk with knowledge and clarity about Jesus' sacrificial death must come down here on one side or the other – on the side of pedagogy which tries to fit him into a cult, or on the side of scandal.

The decision at this point has remarkable consequences. The Christian church, at any rate in the bigger denominations, has always had something of the mystery cult about it. This began when the church entered the Hellenistic world, in which the redemptive call could be heard only as it was sounded by the dominant mystery religions. The new Christian cult became the centre of Christian life. It is true that Rom. 12.1f. had urged people to serve God reasonably in the everyday life of the world and so to be disciples of Jesus who had broken out of piety's taboos into secularism. The reformers vigorously desacralized the church, and made one's everyday life the testing-place of one's Christianity. But it remained a fact that the actual divine service took place on Sundays and was transferred to consecrated buildings which could then become citadels of the faith.

At the best, one's everyday life remained an area open to the radiation of the Christian cult; at the worst, it remained more or less separated from it and was left free to observe its own laws. It was in the antithesis of the French Revolution, and in the continuing effects of romanticism that cultic thought grew increasingly in German Protestantism. The ecclesiastical year never ceases to describe its apparently inviolable circles, telling us that Jesus' fate is the fate of all time, and that we must repeat it and meditate on it, at least in emulation. Here the central mystery is still, on Good Friday and Corpus Christi, in the Mass and in the Lord's Supper, the symbol of Jesus' sacrificial death and its results, which, uncomprehended, grips the participant and brings him into the heavenly world.

We ought to recognize and concede the pagan antecedents of all these sacred matters: Jesus the cultic God, the holy year as the backbone of the calendar and of life, the priestly office which makes the rest of God's people the laity; the holy place which is to be approached with pious awe and is separated by thick walls from the world; the ceremony which brings us into the company of the angels and saints. That is how the church is seen everywhere today by believers and unbelievers. A person's membership of it is decided by his either participating in it or not knowing what to make of it. We have to see before us him who walked the country roads of Galilee and Samaria to Jerusalem, with no home of his own and associating with everyone, if we are to appreciate the far-reaching contrast between the beginnings and the present day. If he had wanted to have this present-day situation, he could have founded a sanctuary such as the Qumran community in the desert and sent his missionaries out from there. In that case the cross itself would hardly have been needed; neither Jews nor Romans nor Greeks had any objection to a new cult. But there must be something wrong with our set-up if we are landed in such a contrast to Jesus himself; we cannot justify it with reference to Golgotha, Easter, and Pentecost if it involves the loss of his reality and his own self. None of the churches wants to hear that the world is no longer being bothered with cults, but that in any case it would find him thrilling, aggravating, and liberating, if it could only get a sight of him. It knows all the facts about salvation. But does it know Jesus? Do we know him? Is it not the real plight of the church today that Jesus has been unknown through the Christian cult? Ought we not to demolish the walls of our ghetto so as to get back to him ourselves and to make him known to others? Would that not be a new Pentecost from which the Spirit would flow out over the earth? Would it not be the Christian repentance (which always means returning) that is currently required of us? Would not any theology that seeks to pave the way for such returning deserve to be taken seriously instead of being treated as heresy? Because the call of his freedom is forgotten, we are experiencing the Babylonian captivity in the modern world.

Even the writer to the Hebrews did not want the new earthly cult; in fact, he declared expressly that since Golgotha all cults, holy places, and priestly duties have ceased to exist; and in this he agrees with Paul. According to him, true divine service takes place when the Son intercedes with the Father for us, and when God's people keep faith on their earthly journey by remaining together under the voice of their Lord. Now there exists a Protestantism which, although it is not specially interested in cultic things, hangs grimly on to the doctrine of the sacrificial death. There could be no violent quarrel with this, if it were regarded, as it is in the New Testament, as one among several interpretations of the cross. But here an attempt is made to tie us down to one single formula and style of preaching; and that is going too far. We can take our stand on the New Testament and its diversity in not allowing Christian freedom to be made to toe the line in this matter; such a price for mutual reconciliation, and even for the achievement of inter-church fellowship, would be too high. We cannot come to terms if it means endangering Christian freedom, for it is the gift of Jesus, with which faith itself stands or falls. So it is no accident that this is the theme of the Epistle to the Galatians, which is the most ruthless book in the New Testament. As the reverse side and result of the justification of the ungodly, it is the church's fundamental article, from which no other article, let alone a sacred formula, releases us.

But there is no need for the other side here to be inexorable, as the Epistle to the Hebrews shows. It makes two things quite clear. First, the expression 'sacrificial death' comes from cultic language, and is therefore needed only as long as we find the cultic indispensable. The aim here, however, is that, in the last analysis, Jesus is to be glorified as the mediator and representative between God and man. We do not propose to enter into this matter at all. But as to words and formulas, may one issue a theological ultimatum 'All or nothing'? How many differences between confessions, and even in pietism, are patiently borne, not to mention constantly occurring scandals? Would not tolerance be desirable here? Is Christ a legislator who dictates what one should believe, so that the Civil Code is inoffensive by comparison with him?

Secondly, we ought to keep in mind that today the word 'sacrifice' is used and understood only in relation to an outstanding, and indeed heroic, performance. No one can be interested in pushing Jesus into the realm of the heroic; that must not be done in any circumstances. On the other hand, however, we are faced with the difficulty that we in our kind of civilization no longer practise cultic sacrifices; at best we simply know of them historically, and at worst we associate them with ideas of magic. What is more, all these sacrifices are intended to elicit God's favour by a pious deed. That is true, even of the Old Testament, although they are explained by divine initiative and gracious permission. In regard to these, too, the New Testament declares that God reconciles himself with us, and cannot be reconciled by us through any human act. As long as the practice of offering sacrifices was openly maintained by Jews and Gentiles, one could say, as in Hebrews, 'That has been surpassed, fulfilled, and finally ended by Jesus'. Today such a comparison has lost its compelling force, because our environment does not give us the direct practice of sacrificial offerings. Only the initiated can supply them from their knowledge of the Old Testament.

So, from whichever angle we look at the problem, the matter is never as clear as it should be to present-day people. If we insist on the precise formula, we merely help to keep alive the pious language of Canaan, and give outsiders the impression that some mysterious happening is involved, so that again they regard the church as a mystery cult. For better or worse, we shall have to take leave of the formula with which the New Testament has made us familiar, if we have any concern for the clarity of the gospel and its intelligibility to the present generation. We may do so if it is of the utmost importance that we should see Jesus as our mediator and representative. Anyone who takes a different view should see whether he can justify it. Theological responsibility compels us here to abandon ecclesiastical and biblical tradition.

These considerations are important beyond the range of our present discussion. To anyone who is at all able to recognize essentials, it is clear that the New Testament is not simply a thing that we possess and hand on unchanged from generation to generation. Its character is bound up with the word; this must be translated and interpreted, and it is ours only for as long as we can be continually making it ours anew – with the help of our intelligence. Moreover, faithfulness to its message requires us to become critical hearers and consider whether we may still use the same words to express what was then intended. We have to combine this with what we were able to learn from the theme of the divine pedagogy and its christological culmination in the Epistle to the Hebrews. We cannot even get through without criticism of the content of New Testament passages. Anyone who speaks of God's pedagogy in a way that is detrimental to christology must himself expect to be corrected, even if he is a biblical author. Even the Scripture must give way to the Spirit, not vice versa. If we are to get a real understanding of God's word, we cannot make the letter sacrosanct. Whoever reads the Bible differently does not keep Jesus as its Lord and standard of judgment, but turns it into a relic, even if it means understanding nothing and substituting superstition for faith. If we accept this as true, historical criticism becomes an absolutely essential tool of theology. It shows us plainly for the first time the diversities of Scripture, and with them its riches. But at the same time it helps us to separate what is necessary and significant from what is open to question. There is bound to be some risk in the use of this method, but there is risk in all methods, and in life itself. If we wanted to avoid all risk, we should have to want not to have been born.

Lastly, it has to be shown here, although briefly, how things stand with regard to the 'existentialist' interpretation of Scripture, which is a controversial subject today. The Epistle to the Hebrews speaks of the march of God's people in the last days, as John Bunyan did in his *Pilgrim's Progress*, with plenty of mythological images and symbols. Bunyan's story seems a trifle strange to the present-day reader, who cannot simply transplant himself into the world of the seventeenth century. Here the existentialist method can help. It proceeds from the structures of human life, as far as we can discern them. In doing so, we come up against the fact that it is characteristic of our personal existence, as well as of the course of history, to be necessarily on the move; there is no standing still in history. Every generation has to set out anew, and will – at death at the latest, but generally while still alive – founder in its own particular way. We cannot establish ourselves on the earth; we are 'strangers and exiles' here (Heb. 11.13). If we apply the Epistle's message to this universal human experience – i.e., if we interpret it existentially – our text's admonition acquires an uncommon significance for our own time. What human beings can never do, Christians must never even wish to do, namely, build impregnable citadels on earth, take their stand on what is conventional so as to abandon the future for the sake of the past. Every one of us is called every day to an exodus, as Abraham had to migrate from his father's house into an unknown country. Anyone who will not join in the march loses touch with God's people, even if he dwells in temples.

What is true for the individual is no less true for the church as a whole. It, too, is constantly being called on to break camp, and it has to leave behind what was once its gain; otherwise it is ruled, not by the Spirit, but by its own tradition. A continual exodus is the reverse side of Christian freedom. To be free, one must be able to give up what is old, and so answer God's will today and tomorrow. In doing so, one is indeed always going out into the desert, across which one always has to trail to reach the promised land. We see that existentialist interpretation is the very thing that helps to make the message of the Epistle to the Hebrews remarkably applicable to us here and now, even though it may upset us. For it is our misfortune that the church, like the old Adam, is rarely willing to set out and trek across the desert; it would rather stick to the good old ways, even when Jesus, as high priest, calls it to perilous freedom and to a heavenly festal gathering on Mount Zion. The Christian world has continually been getting weary on its long journey through time, and has always been tempted in like manner to apostatize from the faith.

If we turn from Hebrews to the two works written by Luke, we seem to have landed in a different world. Yet the writings are linked together by the same theme. Luke, too, speaks of the church's long road, though not in the same way as Hebrews does. It is characteristic of Hebrews that it speaks directly from the journey, as though God's people were tired out and had lain down for the night in the desert. Luke, on the other hand, puts the fulfilment of the divine plan in perspective. His aim, too, is indirectly to cheer up God's people on their way and admonish them to remain faithful; and so his accounts of the various happenings are much more edifying than those of the other evangelists. But the purpose of his work makes it possible for us to call him the first Christian historian, although we must not apply to him the standards of modern knowledge. He at least genuinely tried 'to compile a narrative of the things which have been accomplished', and he did so, as the prologue to his Gospel puts it, in 'an orderly account'. He did so, too, as we see from his initial words to Theophilus, with the very modern intention of providing information. He is therefore much less a preacher than are the other New Testament writers. So we are justified in calling him a reporter, and sometimes a propagandist of the story of the divine victory. Of course, he expected that the end of the world would come, but only in the distant future, and so he looked backward rather than forward, his theme being salvation history in the course that it had taken. The setting of that theme was the creation and the last judgment, and its reflection of the Old Testament gave it historical depth.

We might wish at this point to consider in detail how the Old Testament was taken into the New; but that is impossible within the limits of this little book, and we have to be content with brief notes to fill the gap. The Jewish Christians of Palestine used their people's sacred writings as a matter of course. As the Jewish Diaspora had by then translated them into Greek, there was no special difficulty in making the Gentile Christians familiar with them. The primary aim was, as the account of the passion shows, to give prominence to Jesus' cross and passion and then to the Messiah and Servant of God, seen as a whole and as an event that God had willed and promised. Things were not difficult till the question became urgent whether and how far the Gentile Christians should be obliged to conform to the law of Moses. For the church to know where it stood in this matter, it had to be decided whether the Gentile Christians were to be integrated, however loosely and separately, as a company of proselytes within the Jewish community, or whether there would have to be a complete break with God's people of the Old Testament. The problems arose first with regard to Jewish practices; for some time their fundamental importance was not realized, and they were then put to the test in their various degrees of feasibility. All kinds of attempts were made to get round the clear-cut alternative, but the Pauline mission made it impossible to beat about the bush any longer. It was momentous for the history of the whole church that the apostle, with much contention, carried his point that the gospel meant freedom from the law, and thereby uncompromisingly separated from each other Christ and Moses, the church of Jesus and the newly developing synagogue.

Now, of course, the problem was bound to arise what the

church's attitude was to be towards the Old Testament. It would be well for us to realize that the question of the canon goes back as far as the first century, and is not an invention of historical criticism. If we are to be candid, we must go further, and admit that even down to the present day the Christian world has not finally settled the problem. If we receive the Old Testament into the canon, ought the law of Moses to be binding on us, as sectarians persistently (and not without reason) claim? But if we exempt ourselves from the Mosaic law – and from much else that we simply pass over quietly – , we no longer accept the Old Testament, but at best only selections from it. By what norm are we to make this selection, after we have decided, speaking generally, against the Mosaic law? Here the church has been wobbling along for 1900 years, with various approaches towards a fundamental solution. It is asserted that God's word is in the Old Testament, too; and such assertion is seldom denied. But in point of fact, no one who claims that the whole of the Old Testament is God's word can opt out of the law.

If we looked this question in the face, fearlessly and con-scientiously, we should no longer be able to charge modern theology with betraying the canon – and therefore God's word! It only makes us conscious of how uncertain the church's atti-tude has always been on this point. It has certainly led to inferences for the New Testament which, as was clear in the Epistle to the Hebrews, is not all on the same plane and cannot be uncritically adopted. Even devout people are so human that the fire brigade is accused of arson. People brush aside what they are incapable of mastering, and do not take it kindly when others stumble over it. Just as many parents fight shy of en-lightening their children about sexual matters, so people simply cover up theological problems and are annoyed with those who remove the veil of helplessness or mendacity. It should be understood that, in matters concerning the canon, we do not take anyone seriously or regard him as competent unless he indicates clearly what one's attitude should be towards the Old Testament, including the Mosaic law. Anyone who is following this discussion must get quite clear in his own mind at this point, before we pass on to the New Testament together.

There have always been at least partial solutions put forward. The first of these, as we have said, was to hear in the Old Testament the prophecy of the Christ, and this interpretation is the dominant one in the New Testament, anything that does not fit in with it being generally passed by in silence. Later, as had already been the case in the Diaspora synagogue, there was recourse to allegory; that, too, is barred but by no means ended – the words of Scripture are given an esoteric meaning for which the reader is not infrequently indebted to his own imagination. Thus the Song of Solomon, instead of being a secular complex of love songs, is turned into a panegyric of the community between Christ and the church, although this involves putting up with, and sometimes even enjoying, a great deal of untheological eroticism. The Epistle to the Hebrews presents us with a third possibility: the Old Testament is used essentially as a collection of examples of virtue rewarded and vice punished. All this can, of course, be combined together; that can be done most easily by toning down the contrast between Moses and Christ in the salvation history, with the Old Testament containing the early history and promise, and the New Testament containing the final history and fulfilment.

This, too, does not go to the root of the problem. In the first place, the Old Testament contains many things that are certainly not a promise and can hardly be accepted as being in line with Christianity. In the second place, there is a Judaism that rejects any Christian interpretation of the Old Testament, and can see in it nothing but its own history. What kind of Christian exposition can there be that still allows Jewish exposition its due place? In any case, that is essentially the line taken by Luke when, unlike Matthew, he traced Jesus' ancestry back to Adam. In the so-called inaugural sermon in Nazareth (Luke 4.16ff.), he made the fulfilment of the Old Testament promise the basic theme, not only of the Christian message, but also of the Lucan narrative. The story of Emmaus (24.26f., 32) brings in the passion and the events of Easter. 24.44 repeats this emphatically, and it occurs again in the conflict with Judaism as narrated in Acts.

It is in keeping with this that Luke, not without good reason and unlike the other evangelists, isolates the parable of the sower when he tells it. In this way it is Jesus, in his work as a whole, who scatters the seed of the divine word and founds the Christian mission. As it is already proclaimed at Nazareth in Luke 4.25ff. that the Gentile mission is its aim, so the same thing is inferred from Scripture and from God's plan of salvation in Acts 13.17ff., 46f., and in biting polemical language at the end of Acts. The formula 'This must take place', which was originally used in prophetic language to foretell the events of the last days, was used in a stereotyped way by Luke to indicate the divine will as announced in the Old Testament promise. Our last and most important point here is that Acts 1.8 does in fact set out the programme of Luke's narrative: 'You shall be my witnesses in Jerusalem and in all Judea and Samaria and to the end of the earth.' That is the sequence in which the story of the apostles is then arranged. It may be remarked that the phrase 'end(s) of the earth' comes from Jewish apocalyptic writings, but was used by Luke in connection with the salvation history to mean the centre of the empire, namely Rome. As that is where his account ends, the Old Testament proclamation of salvation is literally fulfilled.

To sum up: Luke's work is a narrative giving his view of salvation history in its final and decisive phase. Because that is the case, it was Luke who first had the idea of combining in a single work the gospel and the account of the mission, the latter being presented as a history of the apostles. Jesus he regards as the initiator of what was completed by the apostles; and the Old Testament was to contribute by providing that salvation history with divine necessity and the depth of world history. That means that all God's actions since the creation have been marked by consistency and singleness of purpose – that is to say, by an inner continuity. In the course of the ages there slowly develops the kingdom, contemplated and willed from the beginning, and now being manifested in the church.

If our eyes are open to them, we can follow the traces of a wise and omnipotent providence in history; we can do so ourselves as historians. Indeed, according to Acts 2.11, those traces are characterized by God's mighty acts, miracles which not everyone is willing to see. But the controversy with the Jews who crucified Jesus in ignorance, and with the Greeks who worshipped the unknown god, shows that everyone could see them, at any rate if the church revealed the existing mysteries. Thus Luke regards the Pharisees, who acknowledged the resurrection of the dead, as the forerunners of the Christians. One might say that they already had in their hands the key that opens the door of God's kingdom, but they just did not use it.

We have to realize the theological nature of this great sketch. Luke was not simply a person who recorded facts. Where he appears as narrator or historian, he is really a theologian, although his expositors have not always noticed it. Personally I should say that, considering the effect that he has had, he is the greatest New Testament theologian. For he has left his mark, as hardly anyone else in the earliest time of Christianity has done, on the church's piety through all the centuries. God's will does not come to us in the word alone; it can also be discerned in the church's tradition and history in later times. Faith means keeping one's eyes open for both these things, as they provide something on which to base it. In this connection we can rightly speak of saving facts. Of course, it is a question of miracles; but these are verifiable, and are observed again and again with astonishment and dismay by Jews and Gentiles. The world is full of God's mighty acts. Just as they are effected by the Holy Spirit, who is thus the power in the miracle, so he is at the same time the force that motivates salvation history as a coherent whole and makes it recognizable to anyone who is willing to believe. Like the Jews, the Gentiles are able to apprehend the divine activity, because they, too, have before their eyes the miracles of nature and of history. Christian preaching discloses to them the real basis of their religious feelings, and leads from natural theology to revelation. Only the impenitent do not believe, although they could see. The

church becomes the nations' mother and teacher, marking the
fullness of the time in the midst of which we live and which
will at last be followed by heavenly bliss. Its work began with
the twelve apostles who were with Jesus from the beginning
and were therefore at the same time his eye-witnesses. Paul was
their delegate for the Gentile world. When he had to depart,
he left to the elders his testament and his warnings against
false teachers who were to come. So, without any clear pronouncement of it, there is something like an apostolic succession in which the ecclesiastical offices preserve the unity of the
Christian world.

What makes the sketch all the more admirable is that it
is all set out in the form of a simple narrative, as it might be
in an elementary illustrated Bible for poor and uneducated
people. Nor shall we forget how much strength, courage, and
discipline the Christian world has repeatedly drawn from this
account. Everything is so clear and intelligible, and at the same
time so skilful and artistic: Luke relates typical scenes that
sink into one's mind and cannot be forgotten, and he is constantly combining his facts with fine psychological insight and
colourful contrasts. It is true that there are inescapable upsets,
obstacles, menaces, and even martyrdoms. Sometimes it comes
to disputes within the community, and even among its leaders.
But in the long run they end happily; generally speaking, all
are of one mind and at least ready to compromise. The devil
finds it difficult to get a living among so many godly people,
and so he has to call in the services of outsiders and dishonest
people. The Christians have friends even among the Jews, and
the Romans are surprisingly tolerant. Even Greek wisdom,
which makes a relatively bad showing here, is at least prepared,
in its own stronghold, to listen to Paul, who knows how to beat
it at its own game. Over everything there presides, like a blue
sky darkened only by a few clouds, that harmony that goes
with divine guidance. It is as if there were a premonition of the
Constantinian epoch that was to come more than two centuries
later. As in the Christmas story, the angels sing their *Gloria*
over what is happening on earth, where wise and steadfast

men, who are ready to die joyfully for their faith, are defending the heavenly cause. We can understand that this Christianity belongs to the future; it neither copies salvation history nor sets out to make world history. For that is how Luke, in contrast to the writer of Hebrews, sees the long road: it is not the heavenward journey of weary pilgrims through desert wastes, but the unceasing triumphant march, even amid blood and tears, where Christian faith overcomes the world.

This presentation does indeed throw up certain problems that we cannot ignore. We wonder what has become of all the dark shadows in the struggles and distress of Christianity's earliest days. Did not Luke idealize more than is legitimate for a historian, and even for a devotional writer? We can quite well understand that he meant later generations to find in his work a saintly past towards which they are to strive. But did he not make too much of its good side? When we consider our own circumstances and the sometimes shameful state of things in the course of church history, are we not bound to conclude that he describes a paradise that has once more been lost? That has to be paid for, because in idealizing its beginnings Christianity is at the same time idealizing itself; and so it not infrequently goes off into a world of dreams and fairytales. If we are now denied access to it, we lose the comforting and admonitory force of our history. Otherwise we are enticed into Utopia. A saintly past, too, has its dangers; and the less they are noticed, the more far-reaching are their effects. If we set out what may be discerned here in terms of the history of ideas, we may say that Luke for the first time reconciled supranaturalism and rationalism on a Christian basis, being helped in this by his environment. In details, his work is full of miracles, and he notes on all sides the divine guidance of history. While the historian brings both into a pattern that combines heavenly and earthly things in a clearly developing plan of salvation, we can detect a trace of Hellenistic enlightenment such as is to be found nowhere else in the New Testament. Religious Hellenism reckons, as a matter of course, with the intervention of gods and demons in everyday life; but the factor of enlightenment comes in when such a belief in miracles does not regard the world as a chaotic battlefield, but sees even the evil spirits as being allowed to stir up trouble over which providence can triumph all the more gloriously. Thus supernatural and historical events balance each other in subjection to a transcendent harmony, immanent continuity, and historical development.

How could such a mixture of apparently incompatible ingredients fail to captivate people? That is precisely what makes it possible to justify modern ecclesiastical schizophrenia. Surrounded by a seething mass of scientific and technical inventions, people are turning to account in their everyday life all the achievements of civilization. To make up for this we provide room in the religious sphere for the supranatural. A disquieting symbol of this state of affairs is the existence of places of worship, still pointing up to heaven, open to everyone, and, as if they were sacred museums, attended by an increasingly tiny number of people. The claim, which used to have some sense in it, to be a centre of public life, is still clung to, and is tolerated rather than taken seriously by the public. It represents that status of the feast-day which is respected, at best, for only about an hour, since, as such, it is almost everywhere devoted to other purposes. If the Christian world has not lost all sense of reality, it ought to realize this in desperate shame, and confess that the former harmony of the world and heaven has changed, in the course of the centuries, first into an edifying hypothesis, and today into a pious untruth. However many people try on their own account to unite supranaturalism on Sunday with the common round of daily life, that union has crumbled and faded around us. A futile labour of love would like to restore the ancestral house. But here, too, we have orders to leave what is old and has had its day. The metaphysical structure of a pre-stabilized order of things, which is reflected, at least fragmentarily, from heaven in earthly form, is finally broken up.

Even in his own time, Luke could cling to this only because he did not feel deeply enough the offence of Jesus' cross. Of course, he relates the passion story; but he makes it, like Stephen's martyrdom, a matter of a peaceful death and overcoming. Acts declares unreservedly that only the Jews' ignorance and misunderstanding let things come to such a pass. At Easter God rectified this blunder in world history, as he rectifies everything in due course. Luke's proclamation is not a preaching of the cross. It is not even exclusively the gospel of Jesus; otherwise Acts would not fit in so smoothly. It is a missionary history in which Jesus and the apostles follow one another and construct the church. As Luke gathered together various primitive Christian traditions, his account in detail does not always coincide with the general drift. Acts shows, however, that as Jesus is regarded here as the beginning of the last phase of salvation history, so he is at the same time fitted into it. Thus on the plane of the historical narrator there is repeated what we notice in the Epistle to the Ephesians: the church has taken charge of its Lord; he remains its Lord, but he is integrated in such a way as no longer to be its permanent judge. Being exalted, he sits at the Father's right hand and waits for his own people to be gathered to him, while on earth he is represented by the church by virtue of the Holy Spirit and his gifts which have been bestowed on it. He made possible its foundation and world-wide mission; on earth he was the great teacher who worked miracles; dying and rising again, he became its head and the future universal judge. As the offence of the cross is overspread by the gloriole of the resurrected Lord, it is not only ecclesiology that is thrown into relief; Luke, too, is able to make what is for him a very characteristic transition from natural theology to a christology of glory. The development of salvation history joins together all the stages of a long road.

It is now no surprise that Luke did not know what to do about the specifically Pauline legacy. As a missionary to the Gentiles the apostle remains a figure of world-wide importance. In relation to the twelve he is seen as the man who carried out the task that they had given him. His doctrine of justification is superficial. Peter states it in Acts 15.11 as the message of forgiving grace; and that message is still a most moving one in

Luke's traditional material, as for instance in Luke 15. On the other hand, the writer of Acts makes it clear, for example in the story of Cornelius (ch. 10), that in his opinion it is not the godless but the godfearing who are justified. Here, of course, former guilt always has to be forgiven. But revelation may be in reply to religious sentiment, or to the good works of Gentiles. It is no accident that the climax of the Areopagus speech is the quotation, with approval, of the Gentile poet's words: 'We are indeed his offspring' (Acts 17.28). The world that God created was meant for his plan of salvation; that is substantiated by human piety and morality, which prepare the way for faith. But faith is nothing else than the acceptance of the new and perfect religion of Christianity.

Our analysis cannot enter thematically into problems connected with the law in the first period of Christianity. That would provide the counterpart of the presentation of the message of freedom, besides taking us again through the entire New Testament and compelling us to make numerous differentiations. At the same time, we cannot at this point pass them by completely. It is here that Paul's supposed companion reveals most clearly how far he is, historically and practically, from the apostle. For Paul, the law constituted the Mosaic régime of salvation, although on occasion he reflected that that régime was in some degree reflected in the universe as well as in pagan consciences. So the content of the apostle's dour anti-Judaistic struggle was the antithesis between Christ and Moses, because the gospel's exclusiveness could be preserved only if the law ceased to be a compulsory régime for the salvation of Christians. In Luke and the later New Testament writings the conflict was no longer urgent, as they regarded the issue as having been decided long ago, and therefore out of date. There was now no need even to understand the need of it, since Gentile Christianity had put itself beyond the grip of Judaism.

But we come up against related problems from another direction. We can hardly be misinterpreting Paul if we say that he was arguing about man's religious feelings as an example of the question of the law, and that he even recognized them as its centre. Moreover, he felt that the Mosaic law was holy, as an exhortation and a claim by the divine will. But men had perverted it into a means of their religiosity. According to Rom. 1.23 and I Cor. 1.21 the apostle saw in that very religiosity the basis of all sinful perversion, as it presses us to strive after good works and divine recognition. It is the most distinctive mark of a person who tries incessantly and by all means to transcend himself. When Paul takes issue with such a person, he does so under the law, and therefore in that person's religious feelings. Here there emerges the pious person's wish for self-assertion, surpassing that of all others, and therefore necessarily responsible for Jesus' cross, but unmasked here through the cross itself.

Nor can Luke ignore the question of religiosity; but for him and for those who followed him piety is man's highest nobility, as it is the consciousness of being descended from God. As this must be continued by Christian preaching, whether by Jews or by Gentiles, religious feeling must be aroused, encouraged, and preserved. How can this be done? Here Luke makes use of the Judaic-Jewish-Christian inheritance by reducing it to Gentile-Christian terms, thereby making the law of Moses merely the pre-eminent document of moral law. That holds good both for Christians and for the church; and further, it is firmly established for everyone by Jesus and the church's message as something that cannot be bettered. The gospel, which connects with man's piety, no longer contains the Mosaic law as a whole. But it preserves its nucleus and expands it to make its validity universal, and combines with the message of a new morality so badly needed in the pagan world. In this way Christian people form the best possible earthly society of godliness and integrity. Thus they strive to meet the demand for religious and moral perfection that will some day be rewarded by the divine Judge, with its inevitable insufficiency covered by grace.

Who would deny that Luke anticipates here something that Christian history has evolved later, and who will not thank him for doing so? Our thanks are always due to those who are original enough to open out future perspectives and horizons, even if we do not follow them. Who will fail to recognize that here, as if at a trading post, a long road came to an end, so that a new and a longer one could begin? It began with the very early Christian enthusiasm, which imagined itself to be carried away into the heavenly world. Although Paul vehemently opposed this, it was only in the church's crises that he was able to carry his point. It is true that he prevented the Mosaic law from being binding on Gentile Christians; but he did not dispose of the devout man's self-assertive urge at which he was aiming in his struggle against that law. At first the enthusiasts took the place of the nomists. Finally, as F. C. Baur, the brilliant forefather of German critical New Testament research saw, the church mediated between all the disputing parties. It accepted Paul as the missionary to the Gentiles. It accepted the enthusiasts' theology of glory. It accepted from Jewish Christianity the legacy of nomism, based on the Old Testament and reduced to moral law. As these various elements merged together, it finally conceded to a domesticated enthusiasm a permanent right of domicile within its sphere of influence. The religious and moral idealism that can be observed as a mark of Christian faith is nothing else than the early Christian enthusiasm, regulated by the church, but even so a force that exerts its influence throughout the world.

After 1900 years this force, too, has of course slowly run down. It helped to create the secular world, which, however, now feels that it is time to part company and be independent. Paul could say: 'A wide door . . . has opened to me'; and that is taken up with the call: 'Pray . . . that God may open to us a door for the word'. The church's doors are still open. But the doors of the world, through which the church could pass both ways in authority for 1600 years, are being increasingly closed to it. Since Constantine, time has worked on the side of Christianity. Under the pressure of the population explosion, the national and syncretistic religions that have lately flared up, the militant atheism, and the decline of personal piety, we are the first generation to have time against it. What we read in

II Tim. 2.9: 'The word of God is not fettered', can be used as a title for Luke's work, which was meant to proclaim great joy to all people. But if the word of God is not to be fettered, the church has to find it afresh every day and be judged by it afresh every day. If it is turned into the church's self-display, if it gets rigid in its tradition and creed, then the pious man has brought it into subjection to himself, tied it to himself, commandeered it for himself, and changed the call of freedom into the call of a religious party. That began as early as Luke's time, when he identified the gospel with Christianity. Today we are at the end of that road. The only help for us all is that a new Pentecost should rescue God's word from its ecclesiastical, credal, conventionally Christian fetters. The only word that the world will listen to once again is that which was first spoken to the Christian world as it then existed. As long as we are waiting and working for this and wishing to begin the long road once more, we may yet hear the voice of the prophet telling us that 'the time is short'.

6 Those who hunger and thirst for Righteousness

The Revelation of John

The Revelation of John was written at the same time as Luke's work, but there are gulfs separating its message from the latter's. So diverse was early Christianity, even then. Revelation, too, proclaims Christ's victory; but it has seldom won the church's favour, and perhaps for that reason it has been liked all the better by the enthusiasts and sects. In contrast to the Pastoral and Catholic Epistles, it preaches Christian freedom with tremendous force, though in a most surprising way. This has two distinguishing features. First, nowhere else in the New Testament is the hatred of Rome, thinly disguised as Babylon, expressed as loudly as here, where it matches what we know to have been felt by the Zealots, and may assume to have been present among many subject races within the empire. That hatred contrasts with the prevailing practice in the New Testament of presenting Caesar's representatives in a favourable light. That is so, for instance, in the account of the passion and in Acts, but also in Rom. 13, and in the advice in I Peter 2.13ff. and I Tim. 2.1f. to intercede for all those in authority. The hatred is understandable, for Revelation was written at the time of Domitian's persecution of the Christians at the end of the first century; and in such times sweetness of temper may desert even the Christians. Even so, it is quite exceptional, in the New Testament setting, for Rome to appear as a beast out of the abyss, and for Christian freedom to be unmistakably combined with a politically revolutionary attitude.

The second surprising element in the message of Revelation is the preaching of repentance and judgment to the whole church, particularly as in the letters to the seven churches, which represent the church as a whole. To find such severity we have to go to Old Testament prophecy and to Jesus' lament over the scenes of his early ministry. The announcement of the judgment goes so far as to make the history of the church end in the graves of the saints and the people shrivelled up in the wilderness. Thus the expectation that Christianity will permeate the whole world is abruptly changed into its opposite; but generally speaking, this is disregarded, as if the New Testament everywhere promised world conquest as the ultimate goal of salvation history. This, too, demonstrates how arbitrarily we deal with the Bible when it does not gratify our own taste and throws our hopes back at us. We may well have reason today to keep firmly in mind that the matter is not quite so simple. Christ's victory is indeed acknowledged everywhere in the New Testament. But that victory is achieved, at least according to Revelation, only after the Antichrist has won his complete victory over the world, and Christianity, decimated over the graves of its martyrs, is reduced to the direst straits.

Of course, we must allow for the fact that this pronouncement is in both cases overloaded mythologically. Nor can anyone with any historical sense deny that the seer's prophecy has not come true as he thought it would. In the first three centuries Rome was to appear to many thousands who had to suffer under it as the beast from the abyss and as the embodiment of the Antichrist, and yet that has not been the final verdict. Christian thinkers and poets were to extol it later for having prepared the way for Christ politically; and within its borders there was to grow up what was known as the Christian West. Nor can there be any doubt that John believed the end with its terrors to be close at hand, although the fact has often been ignored later by people who thought they could compile a Christian history of the world from the book of Revelation. So he was mistaken on both counts, and one can understand why many generations have regarded his work as a sheer phantasmagoria – a view in which orthodox people and liberals actually agreed.

This might be the right place for an unprejudiced discussion of Rudolf Bultmann's programme for the demythologizing of the New Testament. Perhaps anyone who disputes it from the first and on principle will be good enough to tell us what he himself makes of the Revelation of John. He cannot get out of this simply by talking airily about images. No one who takes his stand literally on the biblical account of the virgin birth, the ascension, and the descent into hell can get out of a difficulty here, or in the story of the creation, by any such talk. We must at least insist on his being consistent. If anyone feels so tied to the letter of the text that he thinks the very word 'mythology' is blasphemous, he must not try to undermine this particular text. The seer's visions of the opening heavens and of all that is poured out of them on to the earth are images just as much, and just as little, as the story of what happened on the road to Damascus, or of the baptism of Jesus. There is no doubt that the seer intended to speak of events as actually occurring. It is grotesque that we who advocate demythologizing have to defend him against those who fiercely object to mythology elsewhere in the New Testament. They evidently feel that John went too far. But we will not dispute it if they say that the problem depends on dosage. If they think they have a right to examine us on what we regard as valid or invalid in the Bible, they must allow us for once to turn the tables. It is just not the case that they alone can come forward as defenders of the faith and that counter-questions are ruled out. Anyone who finds mythology in the Revelation of John distasteful ought to be the better able to appreciate that we have like feelings elsewhere. At any rate, he ought not to presume any more on the 'It is written'.

It certainly seems to me just as clear from the seer's work that existentialist interpretation is an indispensable, though by no means an exclusive, means of exposition. Its drawback is that, although it enables one to see the historicity of man, it does not give an adequate view of world history. It will not do for us to reduce world history, as a matter of course, to the historicity of human existence. Revelation shows us beyond doubt that the New Testament is concerned, not merely with human existence, but at the same time with world history. It therefore asks everywhere: Whose is the world? If it did not, it would have no connection with the Old Testament, and what it says about existence would be meaningless. For there is no existence apart from world history, as our own century makes obvious to everyone. An idealistic middle-class citizenry still liked to make intellectual personality the centre of the world, and to interpret history accordingly. The unsoundness of such a view is recognized by Marxism, and could have been found out long ago from the Bible. Man is not simply the agent and the subject of history, for as he unquestionably belongs to nature, so he is also the object and the scene of history as it is enacted. His life is determined, not merely by the individual who meets him, but equally so by all the anonymous powers that we have to include within the larger concept of 'world'. We can no longer be so apolitical that we find it possible to regard world history as an abstract or even a mythological cypher of the historicity of man.

We may say, therefore, that New Testament mythology is necessarily involved here, because the gospel has to do, not only with the individual person's belief or unbelief, but with world history. Of course, it is true that what concerns everyone and is called freeing the earth of demons – i.e., salvation – must be realized by means of the individual. But although it must be grasped in its essence by the individual, it must not be confined, either wholly or partly, to this aspect, or to the personal relationships that are often invoked. The world is more than a web of personal relationships, as the experience of the twentieth century is making clear to everyone. One is thrown, not only on to his neighbour, but into the entanglement of a common fate. Biblical mythology expresses this in its own way, and asserts that salvation and disaster either have worldwide horizons or are pious illusions. Demythologizing must have regard to this aspect in particular; and so, although it cannot dispense with existential interpretation, it cannot be identified with it.

But if that is how things are, we can no longer make a clean break between the gospel and politics, as if the former were entrusted to Christians, and the latter to other people, or to Christians as nothing more than a second-rate instrument. It is true that the conflict between Christ and the emperors does not arise till late in the New Testament. It is very doubtful whether Jesus was particularly involved in the Zealot problem. But that problem was potentially in the air from the time when Jesus converted Zealots and allowed himself at Easter to be claimed the future universal Lord, exalted to heaven. It may be that the conflict between Rome and the church was due to misunderstandings on both sides. One might say that it was inevitable from the time when nascent Christianity recognized and preached Jesus, not only as its cultic hero, but as the true Lord of the earth. For that position was already occupied by the Roman emperor, at least in the Mediterranean area. If the church's message was meant seriously, it was bound to lead to a conflict of legal claims, even if Christians had not the least idea of resorting to the use of force, either for attack or for defence. They had to refuse the emperor honours that would symbolically ratify his claims, and on the other hand they had to ascribe to their own Lord honours that the emperor could not tolerate. That conflict had a depth that the political surface could not conceal.

Whose is the earth? We have again been confronted with this problem. Did not the Nazis carry on their fight against us with the slogan: 'Heaven for sparrows and Christians, earth for us'? How many of us actually accepted it, in spite of the contemptuous method of expression! People did so because they seriously maintained that Jesus' kingdom is not of this world, or because they concluded from a questionable doctrine of the two kingdoms that, for the sake of order, even a doubtful authority had to be allowed to act on its own responsibility in political matters. The result was an attitude that resisted state interference only in church affairs, and elsewhere allowed concessions and compromises up to the extreme limit, and a silence like that of whipped dogs. Did we not wrestle for ten years in our own ranks about whether we should support the Barmen Declaration that no place on earth should be left without Christ's promise and claim? Was not that wrestling more bitter than our sufferings in the political sphere, without ever leading to a final settlement? Did we not find the problem more acute and more cruel than ever after the 20th July 1944? We had once learnt, in church history, that the murder of tyrants, even if it had Christian support, is the wrongful act of morbid fanatics. Apart from a few people who painfully changed their minds before 1944, we should never have ventured to imagine that it could be otherwise. Nor do most Christians in Germany think differently even today, although they have somehow or other come to terms with the events that have taken place, and have kept them out of their minds and consciences as far as they could. Have not we ourselves, who could not follow such an easy road in view of past events, carried those events round with us long after the war, deeply disturbed and unable to get on top of them and resolve them theologically? Did not the whole of our bygone world have to collapse in ruins before a relatively small number of us at last decided to assent, in certain circumstances, to the attempt to murder the tyrant, and to the consequent unavoidable possibility of a bloody civil war? This covers a very wide field which we cannot traverse here or clarify adequately in all its dangers, exigencies, and unanswered questions. What matters is the objective, binding decision that we take personally. That decision is not to be identified with the revolutionary utterances of Revelation, but makes them more intelligible to us than they were previously. They have a theological relevance which is seldom recognized, but which ought to trouble us.

It is grotesque that churches and Christians back away from these questions, either timidly or with the easiest of consciences, whereas for the last twenty-five years they have been discussing all over Germany in deadly seriousness the question of the full or partial ministry of women. In this connection they can plead conscientious scruples on scriptural grounds, and can elsewhere even decline ecumenical community if I Cor. 14.34f. is not properly respected. Here indeed gnats are strained out, camels swallowed, and problems created in which Christian people show themselves as embarrassed as if they were still in a state of medieval patriarchalism. And the question of the relationship between Christ and revolution has been doing more than burn our fingers since the white man's world-domination has been nearing its end. It is easy to find here as much Scripture as is misused elsewhere for squaring one's conscience. The church also has to take responsibility for what it has not done. It is no excuse that, like artful children, we have shut our eyes at the right time, or wailed about the perplexities of the wicked world. The age of the atomic bomb is, in fact, an age of barbarism. Any disciple of Jesus who is concerned merely to keep his own name clean and is afraid to soil his hands reflects a caricature of the bourgeoisie, which in case of alarm pulls its nightcap over its eyes and forgets that its Lord died in no-man's-land on earth between Zealots, although he himself was no Zealot. It is true that the 8,000 crosses that the Romans set up on the Via Appia after the slaves' insurrection are not to be compared to Jesus' cross if one asks about the reason for them. But can the Christian pass them by without recollecting that his Lord, too, suffered precisely that torture? Is there not a community of those who are oppressed and insulted, which goes beyond all guilt, and which Christians cannot evade? Are they innocent if, whether deliberately or not, even if only through their silence, their mistaken respect for the authorities, their pious short-sightedness and narrow-mindedness, they have in the main given way to the tyrants, supported the exploiters, and belonged to the privileged?

That is not to say that they ought to preach insurrection, draw the sword either wantonly or in self-defence, and make revolution the gospel's means and aim. They really have not done that so often that one can raise that kind of bogey and resort to atrocity stories. That always happens when the problem arises of the Christian's responsibility in relation to world politics. But today we have to start from the fact that for more than 1500 years the churches have normally been on the side of the existing ruling order. To that extent they were involved in the wrong, the oppression, the robbery and murder perpetrated by those in power, and not infrequently they shared in the profits. It is not without reason that the revolutions of the western countries have throughout been directed against the established churches as well as against the authorities; and it is no accident that the process is at present being repeated all over the world in the areas of former colonialism. Are we seriously to maintain that we do not deserve to be treated as the proverb says: 'caught together, hanged together' (*mitgefangen, mitgehangen*)? We can do so only by keeping in mind the historicity of existence, but not the brutality of world history and the involvement of the church in it. To keep clear of revolutionaries in order to help maintain the *status quo* is at least as discreditable as it is to rush into the arms of revolution. We must sooner or later recognize this dilemma, take it seriously, discuss it, and at least temporarily and tentatively solve it.

In this we must not even stand still. A crucial particular problem of the complex that we have touched on is that the churches have not only irresponsibly supported the ruling powers and the white man's predominance. They have also at times acted hand in glove with the various nations in such a way as to have been regarded at last simply as their instruments, and to have been able to concur in that view themselves. The false doctrine of the German Christians by no means came to an end in 1945; it simply went underground, just as in America there is a not unimportant connection between segregation and the churches of the southern states. So, too, the nationalism of the European churches everywhere provides a counterbalance, and one of the greatest obstacles, to the ecumenical movement. It would render a service if the so-called Confessing Movement, ('No other gospel') were to play the same part here of guardian of the grail as it does in relation to modern theology. Anyone who has grown up in a national

tradition and has not been able to see the danger that it has
for a long time been to Christianity, anyone who has taken
for granted the official marriage or unofficial partnership of the
two, will not easily free himself from such ties even today.
It is quite beyond dispute that the church serves its people and
has to do so willingly and resolutely, its service always being
indicated by its geographical position. But this close tie with
one's own people is not a distinctive mark of Christianity, but
solely the logical consequence of its obligation to the people
within its reach. If there is anything that we ought to have
learnt from the Church Struggle, it is that false doctrine makes
one particular nation the direct object of Christian service. This
it can be only indirectly, namely, as a political union of people
who are sought after by Christian people and by a particular
church. We are realistic enough not to despise the importance
of such union, and conservative enough not to mislead people
over it in their loyalty and dependence.

However, it must not be a Christian axiom that the state
has a final right of disposal over Christians. Since Abraham,
people have had to leave their own kindred for their faith,
and in the early days of Christianity Jews and Gentiles often
enough had to abandon their native land as well as their native
religion. It is significant that the theme of the Epistle to the
Hebrews is that of the wanderings of God's people, who have
no settled home here. Forty years ago hardly any of us could
have imagined that, for the sake of our faith, we could fail
to support our own nation, or might even take sides against it.
To those to whom the Church Struggle was an even more severe
shock than was the physical distress, such a decision has now
become something tangible, and in the atomic age it might
even be a duty imposed on the church as a whole. Here, too,
it is a matter of not being bound any longer by a centuries-old
tradition, and of being ready for an exodus.

Of course, the objection will be raised to these arguments
that they are extreme and cause unjustified anxiety. But Christian freedom can no longer be called to order for the sake of
peace and quietness. We neither wanted nor sought this

development, but having been forced into it, we cannot now cancel it. Today we can no longer ignore the fact that all life is involved in world-wide politics, and that this also affects Christians. We may well cherish national sentiments in the church where we are competent to do so; but we Christians in Germany ought no longer to offer up incense or any sustenance at all to nationalism. Anyone who has not become an extremist in this matter has slept through the last forty years. It would do him good to read and re-read the Revelation of John, which, like the Epistle to the Romans and its message, is wonderfully up-to-date in all its mythology. Patmos is not an idyllic haven of rest for retired scholars who look back on a hard-working life of piety and integrity, and who, fatigued and already half withdrawn from the madding crowd, give themselves up to all kinds of dreams. Patmos is the place for exiled rebels deprived of their eager activity, and with every idly spent hour burning into their marrow. For over there on the mainland world history is moving, and the churches are spent and either do not see it or try to come to terms with it. They praise Christ as the Lord of heaven, and do not hear him saying to them: 'The world and all that is in it is mine.' They know the first commandment, and they think it is enough if they keep themselves unspotted from the world, although the Antichrist has to be faced squarely if one is to keep alive. They take comfort from the resurrection, and do not know that it begins here and now with the sovereignty of Jesus in the midst of his enemies and with the glorious freedom of God's children who, being ostracized, despise the mark of the beast under the *Pax Romana*. They suffer as though that were not exactly what they are called to do. They ought to make common cause with all those who are oppressed, insulted and appealing in vain to the tyrants, they await him who tramples underfoot the arrogant and the unrighteous, who writes on the wall of Belshazzar's palace while the great feast is at its merriest, and has long since sent out his apocalyptic horsemen. Visions torment the man who can now do nothing but cry out to awaken those who are asleep, to arouse those who are idle, to strengthen those who are exhausted, and to confront with the judgment those who are secure. Mythology helps to set out salvation and disaster in their world-wide scope. Apocalyptic is the language that tells us that the decisive hour is now striking, on which all the future on earth and in heaven depends. Christianity has to take notice of earthly things if it is to be worthy of its call to heavenly things; it must die if it is to live.

For the divine judgment begins at home, and grace does not diminish the Judge's stature. According to Rev. 5, the crucified Lord is the enigma of world history, the central point in the heavenly throne-room, the object and recipient of all the homage of the powers. The fact of belonging to his dominion marks the disciples on earth with his cross and seals them as with the stigmata from the wrath to come. But even so, one is not relieved of present fears, but is plunged into them sooner and more deeply than others are. Jesus' cross consigns its bearer on earth to martyrdom, from which he can be safe-guarded only by the mark of the beast. If the outlook of Revelation was described above as revolutionary, we must not over-look the particular character of those revolutionaries. They fight, not to achieve power, but because they have to become like their Lord. Their wish is, not to conquer the world, but to defend their Lord's claim to the earth, and they die in doing so. Their aim is not the overthrow of the existing order, but the testimony that he who makes all things new is on the way. They are nothing else than the Creator's deputies in a world given to apostasy, and so they have to deal with those who have set up in their own name against their Lord, who do not regard power as a mandate from the Creator, and who therefore misuse it. Thus far, Christians who accept the call to resistance are not simply witnesses to God's reign and tokens of its realization. They are at the same time representatives of a misused creation, the spokesmen of all who are oppressed, the people of the desert who remind everyone that Egypt must be finally abandoned, and that salvation is to be found only in the exodus.

The theme of Revelation is also that of Romans, according to which God's righteousness and man's salvation coincide. God must make good his authority in us if we are to be helped, for there is no real *Lebensraum* for the creature except with the Creator. Because Christ brings together once again the Creator and the creature, he is our Lord, and his rule means grace for those who accept it, and judgment for those who oppose it. As the crucified Lord he brings together God and man, because otherwise he cannot overcome our pride and despair, and God (even if his work were that of continuously raising the dead!) remains far from us. So there is no difference of theme between Revelation and Romans. The fact that Paul is more concerned with anthropology, and that Revelation is stronger in mythology, represents a variation, but it does not change the theme, although it has a theological relevance. With the seer it is a matter of giving our everyday life a perspective of world history. Any such concern repeatedly causes the apostle, too, to use mythological language. With his anthropology, on the other hand, he stresses more strongly the reality of salvation in the Christian's daily life. If Revelation sometimes takes over Jewish tradition too plentifully and too uncritically, that is because the author is human. Historical criticism is not surprised at this, although it certainly need not swallow everything that other times found acceptable.

The real difference between Romans and Revelation is that Paul, who was in contact with Hellenistic enthusiasm, laid more stress on the effective realization of salvation. The seer remained more of a Jewish Christian in that he saw the world's resistance and the tyrants' persecution so clearly that he regarded the dawn of salvation and the reign of Christ (both of which he readily and unreservedly acknowledged) as an anticipation of future perfection. 'The kingdom of the world has become the kingdom of our Lord and of his Christ' (Rev. 11.15) is for him the exultation of the last day. The faith and patience of the saints, on the other hand, have to live for the time being while their Lord is hidden and the Antichrist is in full view. If we can be clear about this, we see that Revelation remains within the horizon of the first and fourth beatitudes,

and that it is in the position of those who wait and who therefore watch and pray for God's righteousness with the first
petition of the Lord's Prayer.

We have reason to let ourselves be recalled to such a position after the official church has for 1500 years been preferring
realized eschatology, or even trying to represent it. Anyone
of ordinary intelligence can see that more has been wrecked in
the last fifty years than had been built up in ten centuries. One
does not have to be a prophet, or see spectres, to be convinced
that in the Third Reich we had only a foretaste of what is
awaiting us. Not only the orthodox church, but every official
church, defends the immaculateness of Christianity as a whole,
no matter how many particular stains and blemishes it dis-
covers and admits. So not only the orthodox church but every
pious community persistently ignores the message of the letters
which indicts and judges the whole church, although that
message ought to make our ears tingle. There will yet be many
lampstands overturned in the holy place, and the present
guardians of the grail have no inkling of it. They play at war
where that can be done cheaply, and will be surprised when
death becomes a large-scale reality. To have mastered apocalyptic jargon means nothing in respect of theology and conduct,
and mere shouting gets us nowhere. Trouncing other people is
a doubtful form of repentance. A summer stay in Patmos is no
substitute for the driving force of the seer's experience, and it
obscures his insight. A complete self-satisfaction dominates
ecclesiastical piety, and covers up the poverty, nakedness, and
shame that is even now being pilloried by the illustrated papers.
In spite of all its activity, the Christian world has withdrawn
into its own private room and barricaded itself in so effectively
that it can generally no longer hear when today's hour strikes.
Its flesh creeps whenever war is threatened in the Middle East,
but meanwhile it warms its feet at its own hearth. If only we
could get away at last from the suffocating atmosphere of
provincialism, where one cannot now get a breath of fresh air,
and certainly not a breath of freedom! Who is to think inter-
nationally, if not those who preach God's reign on earth?

Even in Protestantism, the incense of the mystery religion shuts
out our view and gives us no freedom of thought or action.
What is the extent of our solidarity with all those who are
downtrodden and who have been murdered by tyrants? How
deeply are we moved by the cries for avenging justice, which,
after all, have a legitimate place in the Bible? How much do
we hunger and thirst for righteousness, which not only restores
the dead to life, but proclaims a new earth and has chosen us
to prepare the way for it? We have a vast amount to learn
from the Revelation of John, which, for those of orthodox and
liberal views, has never properly fitted into the traditional
system. For above the place where it puts us is the superscrip-
tion: 'Those who hunger and thirst for righteousness'. That,
however, is nothing else than the reverse side of Christian
freedom in its reality on earth, and of genuine sanctification
that must be practised every day.

7 Freedom under the Word

The Gospel of John

Once more we turn over the pages of the New Testament, which are so richly varied that we never finish with them. Once again we hear the challenge of freedom, coming from the time of Revelation and, more or less, of the Pastoral and Catholic Epistles. In doing so we get another point of view, which, however, takes us back to where we started. The Johannine problem is so complicated that we shall not enter into it. On occasion, one may read the Bible in such a way as to dwell on a particular passage, and from it look out over the country as if no other view existed. Here the call comes to us with unsurpassed conciseness: 'The truth will make you free' (John 8.32). It is worth while to consider this one sentence, and from it to trace our way once more to the central point of Jesus' life and of Christian preaching. The important thing is – and it is not very difficult – to sum up the ground, content, and object of faith. John takes up the message of Mark's Gospel: Jesus brings the freedom of Christians. In John, too, this is attested by the miracles which, not by accident, end in the raising of Lazarus and justify the enthusiasts in saying that even freedom from death has come. Freedom from the temple and the law, for which Stephen was put to death, is now so taken for granted that there is hardly any need to talk about it any longer. In John 15.15 the disciples are explicitly addressed as friends who are no longer servants. Their joy is complete, and, according to the closing words of the farewell discourse (16.29f.), they have no need to ask any more questions – all things become clear to them.

Equally straightforward is the ground of this freedom. The truth that creates it is Jesus himself, for he says: 'I am the way, and the truth, and the life'. So, in a nutshell, his entire promise for his own people is that he will send the Spirit of truth to guide them. Both these statements indicate that the Spirit will remind the disciples of everything that Jesus has said – that is, of Jesus himself – and will keep them close to him. Finally, it is exemplified in Jesus personally that the truth makes one free. His passion is nothing but the clash of freedom and unfreedom, and the victory over the world, as was repeatedly demonstrated in the preceding part of the Gospel. So there is nothing whatever here to trouble one's understanding, though the church does indeed like to represent Jesus' speech and conduct as mysterious, obscure, and incomprehensible, so as to be able to turn faith into a work of pious blind acceptance. Nevertheless, faith does present difficulties here, though they arise, not in theory, but in practice. It is difficult to remain close to him, and so it has to be incessantly talked about, and true faith is described as being continually with Jesus. That is why he calls himself the way; in his company we never reach the end, as he takes care that we are always on the road. Discipleship is not something that can be learnt for all time, but a permanent apprenticeship in the school of Jesus. All things become clear if we ourselves become free, if we stand in the love and friendship of the Master and of God, so long as we follow him and remain close to him. That, however, is the one fundamental condition: we must be bound to him and by him. The disciple will never be free from him without at the same time losing all freedom.

That sounds edifying, but it is highly polemical, as is shown by Jesus' many controversies with the Jews as representatives of orthodox piety. We have reason to suppose that in those talks John provided the church of his time with a mirror that we are still to use. The real problem of his Gospel is that its message is extremely concentrated. Of course, all the other New Testament writings have for their main topic Jesus who is the Christ. But they develop it in such a way as to bring into view heaven, earth, and hell, as is most obvious in Revelation. In contrast to this, John is concerned with one theme only, which he continually varies: to know him is life. That, then, is the one question that he asks his readers: Do we know Jesus? Everything else fades into twilight and darkness; it loses its importance and is pushed aside. Men and the world become important only so far as they have to do with him, just as God is made known to us only through him.

We need to keep this in mind in today's ecclesiastical discussions. Again and again one gets the impression that what matters is how much one believes and does not believe. Every genuine heresy-hunter has ready a whole catalogue of questions with the prescribed answers, by means of which he can judge of the other person's orthodoxy. This method was not invented recently; it is as old as the church itself, and inquisitors have always found it an indispensable tool. Thus in the attempt to banish justification by works, the flock is kept in leading-strings, while no one notices that this means that justification by works is being carried to extremes. The sin that one commits in doing, or not doing, this or that is venial; but woe to him who does not say Yes and Amen to everything that is in the Bible, is believed by the church, and is included in dogmatics. Sin has its headquarters transferred to the head, and it expresses itself by independent thinking. The fact that that is a purely academic way of looking at things does not now trouble anyone. Protestantism, which came into being with professorial co-operation, has become professorial, at least everywhere in Germany, even in congregational piety. A man's right thinking is the standard for assessing what he is or is not worth, and even what God thinks of him. All vices can be forgiven, from gross moral lapses to spiritual indolence, to deliberate narrow-mindedness and physical laziness; what is unforgivable is deviation from correct doctrine. We do not shrink from splitting up churches and denominations, if it is a question of such things as demythologizing and existentialist interpretation. In the good old-fashioned style, we unleash public anger on those who do not read the Bible as we do.

This is no exaggeration. Those who use the stick can assure us, like good patriarchs, that it is done with the best intent and is for the general good. When did floggers not take that attitude? To be sure, those who are at the receiving end judge differently, and have reason for doing so. They may think they deserve to be let alone for a time, after being whipping-boys for many centuries. Would it not be reasonable, at long last, to remember that the Johannine Christ simply asked the prince of apostles, who had repudiated him: 'Do you love me?'. It does indeed repeatedly happen in the life of a Christian that he repudiates his Master. It can be done in the most diverse ways – for instance, by denying the brotherly love that his last commandment enjoined. The criterion by which the Johannine Christ assesses his friends and repudiators is still 'Do you love me?' What do we make of the Bible if we forget this, even if we hold to everything else? How can one muster the melancholy courage, the incredible hard-heartedness, the insipid stupidity, to inflate demythologizing, historical criticism, and existentialist interpretation into such a bogey that Jesus' question takes a back place?

That does not mean that theological controversy is unjustified and senseless. It has its dignity, its importance, and its right to be impassioned, because in it we discuss whether we really and rightly know Jesus. One can only wish that the churches and the so-called laity would take a vigorous part in such discussions, so that everyone might be sure of his faith. But we must neither lose sight of the Johannine Christ's criterion of discipleship, nor try to go one better than our Master. Even if everything is in confusion, nothing is finally ruined as long as men will still follow him, be held fast by him, and learn from him. Perhaps, indeed, some of those in the Christian church – to say nothing of the world – would breathe more freely and feel a desire for discipleship, if the catechism were not always being held under their noses. One can see, even from pastors and teachers, that complete faith is a rare thing, in fact a miracle, whereas pious imagination is a penny a hundredweight. There are no statistics to tell us how many people are kept away and excluded from God's domain by the terror-stricken consciences of a fanatical minority. Instead, there is a record of everyone who fancies his faith to have been impugned, although his faith is as heavily armoured as a rhinoceros. But people stay away from church, not simply because there are too many critical theologians. Even Satan does not always have a finger in the pie. Quite often one can simply no longer hear what one has already heard a thousand times over. The tediousness of Christian preaching is undoubtedly a greater danger to the church than all historical criticism put together; and as long as the Christian world measures faith quantitatively, that will scarcely change.

We might realize, too, from the Gospel of John, that faith does not rest on the so-called facts of salvation. In this respect Jesus himself is the only fact that counts; all the others are candles that light up this one. Today there are so many candles burning everywhere that the sun is no longer wanted above them. Christian faith is not only tightly packed away in dogmatics; it is further surrounded by the wrappings of an obligatory philosophy that is for the most part at least as old as the Middle Ages. Is there anyone now who has the time and energy to untie the parcel so as to get at its real contents? But Jesus is not to be bought in bulk at the market, and certainly not at the pious Vanity Fair. We have to find him ourselves, and we are not found by him till we ourselves have come to him. So theology is one thing, and faith is another; they certainly belong together, but they are not identical. There are many Christians with a wretched theology, and many theologians who are not Christians for all that. Anyone who can no longer distinguish here is making an idol of theology. In the Gospel of John, the Jews argue unwaveringly against Christ with the dogmatic articles of faith contained in their patriarchal inheritance. We can therefore shelve the question of Christ by concentrating on questions of dogma, as is abundantly proved by all church history.

Theologians and church authorities in particular, as well as church members when they meet together, cannot too often remember Dostoevski's Grand Inquisitor. One cannot then forget the dilemma of all the churches concerning zeal for the kingdom of God and the commonplaces of running a concern. It exposes the predicaments in which official Christianity has constantly been involved with the Man of Nazareth, to whom freedom of faith was the most important thing of all: 'For fifteen hundred years we have been tormenting ourselves with this freedom; now it's finished with.' The church has let the tempter show it three powers that make the rebels happy by permanently enslaving their consciences. It now controls those powers for use against its own Lord: they are miracle, mystery, and authority. It is true that Alyosha Karamazov unmasks the truth in the Grand Inquisitor's existence: 'He does not believe in God; that is his whole mystery.' It would be difficult to describe more expressively and bitingly that page of church history which was always there and which can be read everywhere in retrospect. Anyone who can use his senses will realize this from reading the Gospel of John, if he does not regard it simply as the history of an argument with the Jews: There is the church's dispute with Jesus, whom it claims to represent on earth, and whom in fact it often supplants. It must tremble in all its joints when it is confronted with his portrait. No preaching of his resurrection, and of his position of honour as cosmocrat, reveals his sublimity as does the discrepancy between him and his own people. They can save their lives and their pious practices only by continually laying him anew in the holy sepulchre and rolling the stone of their dogmatics over it. They must condemn him as Herod and Pilate did, for he is not simply their Lord, but their Judge, too.

What gives most trouble to Christians of all epochs is neither lack of faith nor excess of criticism; it is Jesus himself, who bestows freedom so open-handedly and dangerously on those who do not know what to do with it. The church always gets panic-stricken for fear of the turmoil that he creates when he comes on the scene; and so it takes his freedom under its own management for the protection of the souls entrusted to it, in order to dispense it in homeopathic doses where it seems necessary. They are allowed to possess this freedom in the form of hopes and feelings, but only in exceptional times may it be turned into action and vehemence, as otherwise it would blow up the church's structure. The church shares with Caiaphas the opinion that it is better that one man should die for the people – and how it extols such a sacrificial death afterwards! – than that the whole nation should perish. Jesus' gift is taboo to it, and his demand is illusory. That is official Christianity's drama right through all creeds and denominations – or perhaps one should say, drama and comedy. For the truth is that he is unwelcome, not only to Gentiles and Jews, but to each of us, and that his presence results in the death of the old Adam in devout people. How can the church have continuity if it gives him a free hand? All the heretics put together cause less trouble on the earth than he does when, instead of remaining an icon, he comes to life and delivers us over to the fire that he came to light. A further aim of ecclesiastical tradition and dogma is to domesticate him, and today all the churches are living on the success of the attempt. How long is that really to go on? In all the confusion of theology his voice is to be heard unmistakably: 'Behold, I stand at the door and knock'; and his way is also being prepared by some from whom it would not have been expected. People who are (in the church's opinion!) not of age, and educated people among those who despise them, break through their incarcerating dogmas to meet him. It is he himself, and not the church, whom they want to hear. Is it crucial that in this case they discover only what they can understand? Ought not the church to be glad, like the bridegroom's friend, that it may await this event? Ought it not to help every such attempt, however unconventional, be thankful for every grain of newly experienced truth, and say in acclamation, 'He even makes the deaf hear and the dumb speak'? After all, the Lord's handmaid wants to be joy's helpmate, not faith's governess. Do we not read that when the transfiguration had reached its climax 'they saw no one but Jesus only'?

The writer of the Fourth Gospel obviously took the view that every generation has to experience the gospel afresh, and

may therefore write it afresh. But that does not do full justice
to the evangelist's extraordinary undertaking. In criticism his
work surpasses that of his predecessors, and he was able to
undertake such a venture only because he knew himself to be
under the constraint of the Spirit that 'blows where it wills'.
Does not that mean that no generation has truly met Jesus
unless it has experienced him in its here and now, in the existing modern conditions, and has set out to make that experience
part of himself? Whether this will be officially recognized, or
at least recommended as edifying and useful reading, is a question in itself. At any rate, pietism has never been reluctant to
tell the story of Jesus of Nazareth from the point of view of
the time of telling. Even with all the risks involved, the aim
is quite legitimate. Only a rigid orthodoxy will necessarily
regard such an attempt with suspicion on the ground that it
can never pay sufficient respect to the ecclesiastical tradition.
It certainly sounds like a challenge when I now say that what
pietism found acceptable ought not to be denied to historical
criticism and modern theology.

Yes this challenge is an inalienable right. Historical criticism
and modern theology give their own account of the gospel that
they have heard and experienced. The church may often be
thoroughly shocked by it. But when would a gospel have failed
to shock people? In many respects, too, this Gospel may seem
provisional and open to doubt. Well, John himself knew that
'the world itself could not contain the books that would be
written' if one tried to report everything that Jesus did. But
when would a gospel ever have given a complete and accurate
account of Jesus? After all, he is always greater than his witnesses and reporters. This little book is a result of historical
criticism and modern theology. Was not the challenge of freedom necessary, and where does it resound more clearly today
in the Christian world? Would it not be more fitting just to
listen to what we have to say and what we seldom hear at
church, instead of demanding that we keep on reproducing
what others have said before us? For the word about Jesus, in
so far as it comes from the Spirit, is Jesus' word, and his

miracles do not suddenly come to an end. Every generation, therefore, testifies anew with its eyes and ears to what has been happening ever since the days of John the Baptist in Jerusalem, Galilee, Samaria, and as far as the ends of the earth. The apostles do not create the gospel; on the contrary, it is the gospel that produces the apostles.

The church's tradition and the assertions of dogmatics aim at helping us to see Jesus aright. But they suffer from the fact that they show him as our fathers and past centuries saw him. He is continually coming to us again in changed circumstances with the question 'Do you love me?' Truth, indeed, is not what we make of him, but he himself; and every acknowledgment of it is prefigured in Peter's answer: 'Lord, you know everything; you know that I love you.' Has the church any other task than that of making room for such a question and answer? He is the way. We have never done with him, and today many a man who can no longer find him in the Sunday service is on the way with him. Have we, who ought to prepare the way for him, the right so to limit access to him that no one can come to him without our consent and supervision? In that case one is better off among the heretics, who see Jesus himself and want to abide by what he himself has shown them. Is Jesus the church's criterion, or is it the other way round? Theologically we shall probably have to consider what are the limitations to which we are subject in trying to see him rightly, as was the case with Paul and the enthusiasts. But he is not subject to theological limitations when he performs miracles. Above all, theology, too, will learn from him to allow freedom, instead of opposing those who want to hear him and have heard him in their own way. Under his word we become free, and the comradeship of free people grows up, as in the New Testament, beyond all kinds of theological disagreement. It ends only where he himself is lost to view, where he himself cannot get a hearing above the ecclesiastical set-up. Can we hear the parable of the sower in such a way as to realize how often the seed is choked by Christianity?

Now we are back at the beginning. The beginning was Jesus

Christ's freedom, and that is where it must always end, if he is to reign. The fact that he is risen means first and foremost that he becomes present to us with his word, as John's Gospel preaches in its doctrine of the Spirit. Today it is regarded as heresy when Bultmann takes up this gospel message and expresses it by saying that Jesus has risen into the word. One may differ about the meaning of this formulation; but can one deny its rightness without running the risk that over a philosophical assertion – there is a life after death! – his presence and sovereignty may founder in a dogmatic compendium? Is there for us today any resurrection of the dead except through his word, which takes sovereign possession of us? Is John 5.24 no longer valid: 'He who believes my word and him who sent me, has eternal life; he does not come into judgment, but has passed from death to life'? What is the good of a doctrine of resurrection which does not begin and end by seeking resurrection in him, finding it with him, and on that account alone looking out beyond one's own grave? Is not the greatest thing, in life and death, the fact that he came to us and that we heard his voice? What is eternal life, if its content is not simply that we know him and the Father who sent him? How can we become truly free if we do not find our Lord and regard this as our supreme happiness? Dogmatic convictions can never be a substitute for this.

Unfortunately, things will go on as he regretfully described in the parable: the children sit in the market place and quarrel about what they shall play at. Some are for a wedding, others for a funeral; and when the voice of wisdom calls its children to itself, its voice is lost in their quarrelling. Is that not also true of the church in its theology and practice?

Epilogue

The power of Christ's resurrection becomes a reality, here and now, in the form of Christian freedom, and only in that. That reality is opposed on earth by anything that stands in the way of Christian freedom, and only by that. These assertions may sound provocative, and no doubt they are provocative in the same way as and because Christ's resurrection is a provocation of the earth. None the less, they may claim validity as necessary and essentially correct theological statements. Anyone who is inclined to say that they are obviously exaggerated, one-sided, and questionable must not mind being asked in return whether he really knows about Christ's resurrection, or whether he may not be concerned simply with the Christian and non-Christian philosophy of the conquest of the grave. I entirely agree with my opponents that the preaching of the resurrection is at the centre of the present ecclesiastical dispute. But the reason why the argument has hitherto been so confused is that it has not so far been clear whether we base Christ's resurrection on our own hope of overcoming the grave, or our own hope on Christ's resurrection. We must not say that they both come to the same thing, for that is exactly what is not the case. Here, too, theology as a whole is determined by the emphases and the sequence. Our hope beyond the grave can be, but is not obliged to be, based on Christ's resurrection. On the other hand, Christ's resurrection means first, and indeed solely, his sovereignty over the living and the dead. We shall have to speak more of Jesus' sovereignty if the preaching of the resurrection is to be more credible in the Christian world. Unfortunately, however, people have the impression that even now it is more important to disciples what happens to them than what concerns their Lord. That is bad theology, even if it should be typical piety. This little book is not meant only to give guidance on right Christian practice, although some people will judge it as if it were. It is a passionate appeal for a right, that means a christocentric, theology. Here, too, and here only, are made the real decisions for the practice of the Christian life, of our congregations, churches, and the world.

Christ's resurrection means Jesus' sovereignty, and such sovereignty becomes an earthly reality only in the realm of Christian freedom. The earth has no scarcity of lords, and they all demand obedience. Religious commitment as such cannot therefore be the distinguishing mark of the Christian and Christianity; it would show them to be one brand of piety in general. Christ differs from the other lords in that he effects freedom. He does not just call to it; that would be the law of which there are innumerable characteristic forms. Jesus gives freedom. That is what makes him unmistakably Lord and inseparably unites the earthly with the exalted Lord. He was free in that he came to serve, and he remains Lord by serving us. According to Luke 12.37, in fact, the world's Judge on the last day will once more gird himself as a slave. This unprecedented message is the scandalizing and beatific gospel. So the whole life and death of Christian people must be in line with this gospel of the serving Lord, and only thus can it receive the imprint of genuine and unmistakable discipleship. Because Jesus' gift is Christian freedom and we live by that gift and grace of his, Christian freedom demands that we prove it on earth before it is perfected in heaven. It is the sign of those who are called before Christ's judgment seat, and the work that we have to take back to him. It is his work on us and through us. It, and it alone, is the anticipated resurrection of the dead. The world, which needs to be raised from the dead, waits for this revelation of 'the glorious liberty of the children of God' (Rom. 8.21). We have nothing new to tell it and we refuse it the gospel, unless we disclose to its gaze this freedom – not as a utopia, but as Jesus' call and gift. So his gift is handed on by us, and we are guarded against turning our own affair, our personal piety, an earthly business, into our task, into something by which we assess Christianity and the gospel. He remains Lord so far as, and only so far as, his service is passed on through us and brings men into freedom.

The pages of the New Testament have shown us that Jesus' sovereignty is refracted in the most varied ways on earth, and that we are able to grasp it and translate it into action only fragmentarily according to the existing situation. The Lord is more than the disciple – otherwise he would not remain our Lord. What we understand and achieve is patchwork, even under the power of the Holy Spirit, and is clouded by weakness, foolishness, and all earthly characteristics. So the gift remains ours only as long as we are constantly renewing our efforts to reach it, as those who are waiting and receiving the first beatitude. It is enough that we reach out, with the world, for his freedom, and let it consecrate us. But no one can be exempt from that, either during life or at death. No one can be deputized for here, even by the Lord. He is risen, so that we may experience the power of his resurrection and live by it. The call of freedom has been sounded. It concerns every one of us personally, in our place, in our humanity, in this world of ours. The answer to it is the community of the free, and therefore the dawn of a new creation.

INDEX